Cranky Colonials

Pilgrims, Puritans, Even Pirates

by Elizabeth Levy

Illustrated by Daniel McFeeley

with Additional Material by J. R. Havlan

D0955005

SCHOLASTIC INC.
New York Toronto London Auckland Sydney
Mexico City New Delhi Hong Kong Buenos Aires

To Nan, Marge, and Cynthia
and the uncranky times we share.
—E. L.

Expert Reader: Professor Forrest McDonald, Distinguished Research Professor of History, University of Alabama

Scholastic gratefully acknowledges the original inspiration of Terry Deary's *Horrible Histories* series, published by Scholastic Publications Ltd., London, U.K.

0-590-12244-4
Text copyright © 2002 by Elizabeth Levy

Illustrations copyright © 2002 by Scholastic Inc.
All rights reserved. Published by Scholastic Inc.

12 11 10 9 8 7 6 5 4 3 2 1   2 3 4 5 6 7/0

Printed in the U.S.A.
First Scholastic printing, January 2002

www.elizabethlevy.com

Contents

What's So Funny?

History is usually a random, messy affair . . .
Mark Twain, *A Horse's Tail*

The one who tells the stories rules the world.
Hopi saying

Humor and history have a lot in common. They let everybody in on the joke about how funny, impossible, clever, misguided, smart, or silly humans can be and have always been. History and jokes can be horrible and wacky, often at the same time. Horrible comes from the Latin word *horree,* which means to bristle, to make your hairs stand on end. Wacky comes from the Old English word *thwack*, from the sound a stick would make smacking something or someone. So at the very least, the horrible and wacky parts of history will wake you up.

There's a saying that if you don't know your own history, you are condemned to repeat it.

Get it? "Hairs on end?" Oh, yeah. I am one funny roach!

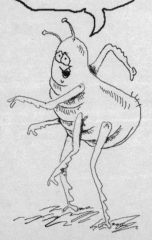

4

I say that if we can't laugh at ourselves, we're in even worse trouble. There are facts and jokes in this book that will make you laugh out loud, ones that will make you grin and groan, and ones that will make you squirm.

While you're laughing at all the jokes and cartoons in *Cranky Colonials,* don't forget the information in this book is real, at least as far as anybody knows. But there is always new information being discovered and new ways of looking at history. Just remember, historians keep learning, and ideas about what really happened in the past sometimes change as often as most people change their underwear.

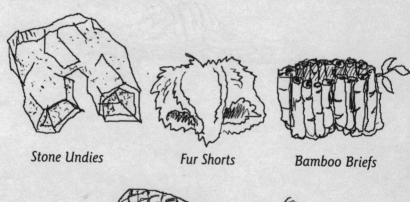

Stone Undies   Fur Shorts   Bamboo Briefs

Grass Weave Thong

The History of Underwear

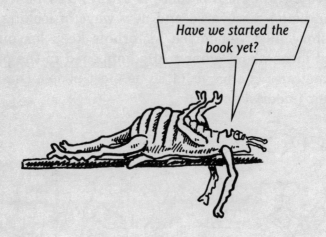

Introduction

The American flag has 13 stripes because that's how many colonies revolted against British rule. Many people think that American colonial history is only about those 13 colonies: Virginia, Massachusetts, New York (originally New Amsterdam), Maryland, Rhode Island, Connecticut, Delaware, New Hampshire, North Carolina, South Carolina, New Jersey, Pennsylvania, and Georgia. But American colonial history also started in places like Florida, Texas, and New Mexico.

Before 1550, the few Europeans who came to what is now the United States were looking for gold. When they didn't find it, they left as fast as they could. But after 1560, Europeans and Africans came to stay, leaving their mother countries behind. A mother country is the original home of anyone who goes to live in another place. Most Europeans chose to leave their mother countries; most Africans were forced to come here as slaves. And the Native Americans did not think for a minute that their "mother" was a European

monarch or that they were a colony. The Native Americans fought to get rid of the Europeans.

Almost half of the European colonials came here as indentured servants. Lots of colonists left for America because they were in debt or had no hope of owning land back in their mother countries. In Europe, usually the oldest son got all the land and the house or castle, too. Wouldn't you be cranky if your parents gave everything to your older sibling and left you nothing? Wouldn't you move if you could? That's what a lot of Europeans did. Some historians call America "the home of the second child."

Still, the Europeans didn't come just to get even with their older brothers. They came for a better life or for liberty or religious freedom (though at first, these colonists meant liberty for people who belonged to *their* religion). You can't understand

American colonial history unless you know something about why so many Europeans left home for religious reasons.

During the American colonial period (roughly, the 200 years between 1560 and 1760), Catholics and Protestants in Europe were at one another's throats, even burning one another at the stake. Catholic countries like Spain and France would go to war at the drop of a hat against Protestant countries like England and Holland.

You dropped your hat. S'cuse me, you dropped your . . . uh-oh!

Meanwhile, England was being torn apart by different groups of Protestants who wanted to reform the Protestant Church of England. Some reformers wanted to purify the English church; they became known as Puritans. Others wanted a separate church altogether. They called themselves the "Saints" because they wanted to be even purer than the Puritans. Then there was the Society of

Friends. Members of this religious group believed that each person had an inner divine light. They believed it was a good thing to quake or tremble in awe of God. Many people call the Friends "Quakers."

These religious differences made the colonial settlements very different from one another, depending upon who settled where. But no matter what religion the colonists belonged to or what country they came from, when they got here they had to build homes and earn livings. Cranky means odd, eccentric, slightly mad, or angry. And you had to be a little odd and eccentric to be willing to brave the terrors of settling in the New World. The colonists were all that, including being courageous enough to leave their homes.

Elizabeth Levy

Elizabeth Levy

Hi, Everybody!

Mel Roach here, returning to you in my capacity as host and emcee of this fine publication. But I'm afraid I've got a little something to admit to you . . . I'm a bit cranky myself. Why, you ask? Well, for one, they made me wear this silly hat. And two, I'm tired! I've been running around this Earth for millions of years now, and every time I think I'm going to have a chance to sit back and relax (and maybe even read a book), somebody's just got to come around and stir things up again. This time, it's some folks that nice lady, Liz, the author of this book, calls the "Cranky Colonials." They came to America from all corners of a place called Europe to try to get their slice of the American pie. Mmmmm! I like pie. . . . Oh, sorry. I got a little distracted

there. Of course, life wasn't a bowl of cherries for those early colonists (or the Americans already here). Cherries . . . yum! Oops, there I go again. Those first cranky colonials got so hungry, they ate

stuff that makes even a roach say "Yuck!" If you want to find out what I'm talking about, all you have to do is turn the page. Go ahead. I dare you. . . .

Chapter 1
Spain and France in First

Colonial history starts with the Spaniards and the French in Florida. Neither really wanted Florida all that badly, they just didn't want the other one to get it, kind of like the way a dog acts with a bone.

Spain was the first European country to have colonies in the so-called New World. As early as 1519, Spaniards had claimed what they called "La Florida," which was the whole southeastern part of the United States, and also the

1562
French Protestants land in Florida and South Carolina

1565
Spanish build St. Augustine, first colonial town

1598
Oñate tries to settle New Mexico

Hello, police? We just got robbed at sword point. They had pointy metal hats, pointy little beards, and they got away in really big boots.

whole Southwest, which they called "Nuevo Mexico." The Spaniards didn't find gold in either of those places. Spain's biggest colony was Mexico where they *had* found gold. But don't call the Spaniards gold diggers, because they did very little digging. They thought digging was beneath them. (Get it?) They found gold and silver in the palaces and temples of the native Aztecs in Mexico and the native Incas in Peru and then they stole it.

1610
Santa Fe founded

1673
French claim Mississippi Valley and Ohio

1680
Pueblo people kick Spanish out of Santa Fe

Other European countries, like England and France, were jealous of all that gold pouring into Spain. They sponsored explorers of their own, but none of them discovered gold. When the English and French couldn't find their own gold, they sent out pirates to steal gold from the Spanish. These pirates often hid along the coves of Florida, Georgia, and the Carolinas, preying on Spanish ships.

Pirates in South Carolina

Jean Ribaut was a French pirate, famous for his long beard. He also happened to be Protestant. Cruising along the coasts of South Carolina, Georgia, and Florida, he stole so much gold for France that the Catholic rulers of France were grateful and decided to let him go to America with 150 French Protestants to start a colony. That way France could get rid of a few Protestants and annoy the Spanish, too.

In 1562, Ribaut knew that Spain thought she owned Florida. Nonetheless, he stopped near Jacksonville and put up a stone column claiming the area for France.

The First Colony: Card Playing and Hanky-panky

Nobody is sure why, but the Timucua people of Florida decorated Ribaut's stone shaft with flowers and carefully took care of it. When another group of French Protestants landed in Florida, the Timucua let them build a fort on their land in exchange for French help against other tribes who were the Timucua's enemies. The French called their town Fort Caroline. They built wooden houses with thatched roofs made of palmetto leaves. The fort had a flour mill, a brick bakery, and a blacksmith shop. The French had shops for tailors and gunpowder makers, and beer makers. What they didn't have was many gardens. The Europeans weren't into planting. They figured the Timucua would bring them corn and beans. They spent a lot of time smoking tobacco with the Timucua and playing cards. Eight out of 10 babies who were born the next year were half French, half Timucua. One of the Frenchmen, an artist named Jacques le Moyne, painted beautiful pictures of the people he met there.

Spaniards Found St. Augustine and Massacre the French

The Catholic Spaniards hated that French Protestants, of all people, were poaching on Spanish land in Florida. The king of Spain, Philip II, decided to send one of his top naval officers, Pedro Menéndez de Avilés, to drive out the French. Menéndez left with 1,500 Spaniards, including 26 women and their families. This was the first time that Spaniards came with the idea of staying in what is now the United States.

The Spaniards arrived with pigs, horses, and supplies to drive the French out and to set up a colony of their own. Menéndez landed on the

Florida coast on August 28, 1565. It was St. Augustine's feast day, so he called his landing place St. Augustine. St. Augustine, Florida, is the oldest European-established, continuously occupied city in the United States.

Menéndez barely stopped long enough to unload in St. Augustine. He and hundreds of his fully armored men marched through a swamp to Fort Caroline — in the middle of a huge hurricane!

I GOTTA start checking the weather reports before I try this stuff!

At dawn, they completely surprised the French at the fort, sticking their swords and pikes through 162 of them.

Menéndez then went back to build St. Augustine. The Spaniards got to work erecting a little wooden fort and a church. They lived in wood-and-mud huts. They were not very happy. They hated Florida's mosquitoes and heat.

The Spaniards soon found out that the Timucua were tough warriors to mess with. St.

St. Augustine, Florida. Castillo de San Marcos National Monument is the oldest European-type fort in the United States. On most days the cannons are fired from the fort and a sound-and-light show, *The Cross and the Sword,* reenacts the city's bloody beginnings.

Augustine never grew into a great colonial center, like Mexico City, as the Spaniards hoped it would. The city was constantly under attack from French and English pirates. But each time St. Augustine was destroyed, the Spaniards rebuilt their little fort, church, and town.

Spanish Missions in Georgia and on Chesapeake Bay

Of all the Spaniards, Catholic priests were the most willing to stay in the New World year-round. They felt it was their spiritual mission to convert the Native Americans. They, often with the help of local Native Americans, built actual missions, too. The missions were a place for worship and a home for the priests. Most of the Spanish missions were just little wooden or earthen huts, but they almost all had a cross built either on the roof or directly in front of the

Seashells Repel Cannonballs

In 1672, after 10 little wooden forts had come and gone, the Spanish got serious about building a real fort in St. Augustine. They brought over stonemasons from Havana, Cuba. The new fort, Castillo de San Marcos, took 22 years to build. It spread over more than 24 acres. Fifteen hundred people could live inside its massive walls. The walls themselves were 12 feet thick and 30 feet high. They were said to be so strong that cannonballs would bounce off them (although no one was in a hurry to test *that* theory!). The walls' mortar was made out of oyster shells mixed with sand and freshwater to create lime; that mortar still holds the fort together today. The bricks for the walls were made out of *coquina*, which means "little shells" in Spanish. More than 50 cannons guarded the fort from its four towers. Despite several attacks during the next 100 years, Castillo de San Marcos was never taken.

Mission impossible waaaaay before Tom Cruise.

Good morning, padre. Your mission, should you choose to accept it: Convert everybody! This sundial will self-destruct in five seconds.

building to show that this was a place where Jesus Christ was worshiped. The priests hoped that the Native Americans would want to come live in the mission compounds with them and learn to speak Spanish and wear Spanish clothes.

In order to gain more converts, Spanish priests moved north from Florida. After building a series of small missions on Georgia's Atlantic seacoast, they moved as far north as Virginia and Maryland on the Chesapeake Bay.

Go West!

Two thousand miles away, other Spaniards were also trying to convert the Native Americans, and they were having the same luck as the Spaniards in Florida. In other words, not much. At least at first.

In 1598, 10 Spanish priests left Mexico with

Cleanliness Not Always Next to Godliness

Geez, that guy stinks to high heaven

The priests wore robes, which they rarely, if ever, washed. Underneath they wore tunics. Most Europeans had few clothes, and no one, priest or soldier, changed clothes very often. Europeans also didn't bathe nearly as often as the Native Americans they met. Native Americans wore fewer clothes, but they usually considered cleanliness very important. Most of the Timucua and their warriors wanted to trade for Spanish guns and metal knives and cooking pots, but they weren't interested in the Spaniard's religion. They found the Spaniards, including their priests, smelly and ugly. (Remember those dirty clothes and unwashed armpits?)

Juan de Oñate, heading for Nuevo Mexico (New Mexico). Most of the other Spaniards with Oñate were *not* looking for souls to save. They were looking for gold. King Philip II of Spain asked Juan de Oñate, one of the richest men in Mexico, to go look for gold in Nuevo Mexico, mostly because Oñate could pay for the expedition.

Let's do the math here: 500 people, 7,000 large animals. Spaniards must like to do some serious eating!

Altogether, more than 500 men, women, and children, including Oñate and his wife Isobel's 10-year-old son, Cristóbal, headed north from Mexico. They traveled in 83 wooden wagons, carefully packed with Spanish jars holding wine, olive oil, honey, and other foods the Spaniards thought were necessary for a good life. And don't forget the barbecues. The Spaniards brought herds of 7,000 cattle, sheep, and horses with them.

Oñate and his troops followed the Rio Grande into what is now New Mexico. Instead of finding gold and silver, they found dusty lands and little to eat. The Spaniards settled deep in the homeland of the Pueblo peoples. *Pueblo* is a Spanish word that can either mean a town or its people. Today, many tribes in New Mexico and Arizona use it as their name for themselves. The Pueblo peoples built homes out of thick, sun-baked bricks that the Spanish called *adobe*. The adobe kept the Pueblo dwellings warm in winter and cool in summer. And that's without central air and heating!

The Spaniards told the Pueblo peoples that they had been worshiping the wrong gods. If they didn't convert to Christianity and do everything the Spaniards asked them, they risked death. The Spaniards insisted that not only should the Pueblo peoples convert but that they should also feed the Spaniards and build new adobe homes for them. Needless to say, the Pueblo weren't exactly lining up for this opportunity. Oñate wrote that the Spaniards expected to pick up bricks of silver, and when they didn't, they got mighty cranky. Okay, he didn't use the word cranky, but that was the basic idea. He also complained that he tried to get the Spaniards to contain their cruelty to the Native Americans, but they wouldn't obey him.

Actually, Oñate himself was no slouch in the cruelty department. When the Pueblo people of Acoma resisted, Oñate was so cruel (hacking off the limbs of survivors) that even his own men complained.

Texas Gets the First Thanksgiving — No Reports of Turkey

Oñate and his troops crossed the Rio Grande into what is today El Paso, Texas. On April 30, 1598, along the banks of the Rio Grande, Oñate declared a day of thanksgiving, a day of feasting and religious activities to celebrate the fact that they had come to a cool river. Oñate declared the site of the festival "El Paso del Rio del Norte," the "pass across the great river of the North." It would later become El Paso, Texas. (The word Texas comes from a Native American word for friend or ally.) For good measure, Oñate declared that all the land watered by the Rio Grande belonged to God and King Philip II of Spain.

> Texas sure means "friendly" to me. Those Texans built me my own Cockroach Hall of Fame in Plano. Stop by and tell a few thousand of my relatives hello for me.

Spain knew that it didn't have enough soldiers or money to control the vast empire that it had claimed: everything north of Florida, and the whole West, from Texas to California. The Spaniards hoped that all the Native Americans would become Catholic, speak Spanish, and be vassals of the Spanish king. Then they could save souls and control the land, too. It seemed so simple to the Spaniards. But most of the Native Americans neither wanted to speak Spanish nor become Catholic, especially since the Spaniards basically wanted them to be their slaves.

The king of Spain wanted New Mexico to be a royal colony with a real capital. From 1609 to 1610, Spain sent Oñate's successor, conquistador Don Pedro de Peralta, up to Nuevo Mexico. Peralta and his soldiers moved into the ruins of one of the small ancient pueblos, known as Kaupoge, or "place of shell beads near the water." It was so named because in ancient times it was probably near the edge of a great inland sea where mammoths had once roamed. Peralta renamed the town *La Villa Real de la Santa Fé de San Francisco de Asis* (the Royal City of the Holy

So you're saying you want to rob and enslave me and you want me to say gracias?

EXACTLY! What do you say?

You Want That Tortilla With or Without Urine?

The Pueblo peoples had their own religion. They believed that the gods taught people practical skills like fire-making, weaving, hunting, and farming and taught them about the spirits in all the earth, in the mountains, caves, rivers, animals, plants, and human beings. The Spaniards often killed or enslaved the Native Americans who rejected Catholicism and went back to their own ways. The Pueblo peoples began hiding their religious ceremonies. They also made little protests, like the time some women of Taos cooked tortillas for a Spanish priest. Those tortillas were made of ground-up field mice and urine. If the priest thought they tasted funny, he never said so.

Taco Gong

ALL NEW
Mouse
&
Urine
Tacos!

ALL NEW
Mouse
&
Urine
Tacos!

Don't think that one's gonna be catching on.

Faith of St. Francis of Assisi). Today, Santa Fe is the capital city of New Mexico, the oldest city that is now a state capital in the United States.

Peralta changed Kaupoge so that it looked like a Spanish city. It had a plaza in front of the huge Palace of the Governors from which the Spaniards planned to rule all of Nuevo Mexico. The palace was built of adobe. It was more than 300 feet long and included both offices and living spaces. Spaniards did go in for some strange decorations — sometimes they hung the ears of the Pueblo people they had punished on the palace walls.

As a colony, New Mexico and its town of Santa Fe grew very slowly. Santa Fe is nearly 2,000 miles from Mexico City, and in 1610 it took six months to travel between these two cities. After 50 years, only about 2,000 Spaniards had moved into New Mexico.

The ones who did move had a pretty good life — and that can only mean one thing: a bad life for the native people. The Spanish forced the Pueblo peoples to build them *haciendas*, which were ranches with adobe-brick main houses. The adobe was usually a foot or more thick so that the houses would be cool in summer, almost as if they had air-conditioning. Today, almost every house in Santa Fe is still made of adobe.

Santa Fe, New Mexico. The original **Palace of the Governors** is now a southwestern history museum. It is the oldest public building in the United States. Near the Spanish mission church is a house that was first built in 1200. Outside Santa Fe, visit **El Rancho de las Golondrinas,** a living museum of Spanish colonial life.

Hey, Who Wouldn't Want to Ride a Horse?

The horse disappeared from North America during the last Ice Age, about 10,000 B.C.E., so

Native Americans had never seen a horse before the Spaniards came. The Spaniards tried to keep the horse away from the Native Americans, because they knew that a warrior on a horse was a much more powerful enemy than a warrior without a horse. For one thing, he's much taller.

But since the Spaniards didn't want to do the work of ranching themselves, they had to teach some Native Americans to ride. These *vaqueros*, or cowboys, often escaped with their horses and taught other tribes to use horses and to turn their new skills against the Spanish. In 1639, some of the people of Taos, New Mexico, stole Spanish horses and hightailed it to Kansas. There, they introduced horses to the Cheyenne, Comanche, Wichita, and other southern Plains tribes. The horse turned out to be a great help in hunting buffalo. Tribes who used to hunt buffalo only part of the year now turned to hunting

buffalo year-round. So much for vacation time. Not so great for the buffalo, either.

Spanish Kicked out of Santa Fe

Around 1650, New Mexico and the whole West went through a terrible drought. Everyone began to starve. The Spaniards were forced to eat their leather boots soaked in water. The Pueblo

No, thanks. I'm more in the mood for Chinese.

peoples had even less to eat. Popé, a shaman or religious leader from the Tewa Pueblo, preached that the Spaniards had stopped the rain. It was time to go back to the old gods and pray for rain. The Spanish priests warned the Pueblo peoples they would go to hell if they returned to their old ways. Popé and other shamans were thrown into a dungeon under the Palace of Governors and

Excuse me . . . pardon . . . ¡hola! *Little help, please . . . I think I hear my cell phone!*

How to Bake a Human: Or How to Make a Spaniard Quake in His Boots

Nearer to Santa Fe, nobody got better at using horses than the Apache. They had been raiders and warriors before the Spaniards arrived. If Apaches on foot had been feared, Apaches on horses made the Spaniards quake in their boots, especially after Spaniards started raiding Apache camps for slaves. The Apache raided back. Sometimes the Apache would spare Spanish women and children and adopt them into their tribes. But they would often torture the men. They might spread-eagle their victim over a cactus or bury someone up to his neck with his eyelids cut off. The victim would be left to bake in the hot sun.

whipped. Three of the shamans were hanged. One killed himself.

Seventy Pueblo warriors marched into the square in Santa Fe in front of the Palace of the Governors, basically saying, "If you don't free our religious leaders, we'll join the Apache." The Spanish were so afraid of the Apache that they released Popé and the other shamans who were still alive the next day.

Once free, Popé spent five years secretly uniting the Pueblo peoples and making peace treaties with the Apaches and the Diné (Navajo). In 1680, Popé and his warriors attacked the Spanish priests in the pueblo of Taos and the Spanish ranchers and their families in their haciendas. They killed as many as they could. The Spaniards who survived fled into Santa Fe, thinking that they'd be safe in their capital. The Spaniards huddled together in the plaza and the Palace of the Governors. Popé and his troops cut off water to the plaza. The Spaniards began dying of thirst. On August 21, 1680, the Spaniards surrendered. There were about a thousand of them left.

Men, women, and children, all the Spaniards thought for sure they'd be slaughtered. To their surprise, they were not attacked when they marched out. Popé let them go. The surviving Spaniards straggled out of Santa Fe, passing burned-out haciendas. Hundreds of Spaniards lay unburied in their gardens and in the road. Every church lay in ruins.

The Spaniards Settle in Texas for Good

The Spaniards struggled south through Texas, trying to get back to Mexico. Again, they stopped

The original **Yselta Mission** in **El Paso, Texas,** was washed away in 1740 when the Rio Grande flooded, but it was rebuilt, and you can visit it today.

on the banks of the Rio Grande, about 12 miles from what is now downtown El Paso. Some of them stayed, started a new settlement, and went to work building a permanent mission, Yselta. Soon they had a string of missions. This was the beginning of the Spanish settlement of Texas.

Spanish Colonists Back in New Mexico to Stay

For 12 years, the Spaniards stayed out of New Mexico. In 1692, however, they returned, coming up from Mexico under the command of General Diego de Vargas who had fought in many European wars. Vargas retook Santa Fe and moved into the Palace of the Governors. Seventy rebel leaders were shot in the town plaza. More than 400 Pueblo men, women and children were sold into

We're baaaaaack!

35

slavery. The Spanish rebuilt Santa Fe, taking over many of the original Pueblo houses and covering them with new adobe. Santa Fe would remain the Spanish capital of the West for more than 200 years. A fiesta was held in 1712 to celebrate the Spaniards' return to Santa Fe; that Santa Fe Festival is still held every September.

Even with a fiesta every year, not many Spanish colonials moved into New Mexico. Spain could never convince a whole lot of its people to move up from Mexico or to come over from Spain. And they weren't the only European country having that problem.

France: Great Food, Lousy Numbers

During the Colonial Era, France was one of Europe's most powerful nations, and it's always been famous for its good food. Around 1600, France had a population of 16 million, compared to 8 million in Spain and only 5.5 million in England. As early as the 1520s, fishing boats from France sailed across to the rocky coasts of Maine and Canada. They couldn't believe how many millions of codfish were just waiting for them. The French would sail over for the summer months and build huts onshore. All summer long, they'd dry codfish fillets, slicing, salting, and sticking tons of cod in barrels that they took back to France and sold in fish markets. It was a smelly start.

I . . . am a codfish. Most of my friends are codfish. I know codfish! I'm telling you, we were NOT "waiting" for the French!

The French didn't have a real colony in North America. Then in 1603, Samuel de Champlain made his first trip to the New World. In 1608, Champlain began to build New France's capital city, Quebec, on the St. Lawrence River in what is now the province of Quebec, Canada. He sent some of the young French boys with him to live with the Huron of the area and learn their Algonquin language.

During the next 30 years, Champlain crossed the Atlantic 29 times, logging more than 100,000 miles, trying to set up New France.

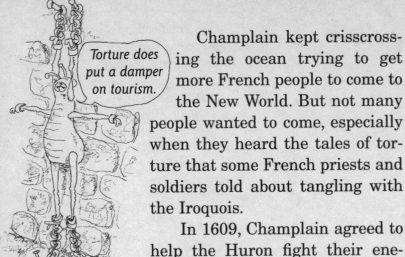

Torture does put a damper on tourism.

Champlain kept crisscrossing the ocean trying to get more French people to come to the New World. But not many people wanted to come, especially when they heard the tales of torture that some French priests and soldiers told about tangling with the Iroquois.

In 1609, Champlain agreed to help the Huron fight their enemies, the Iroquois, in what is now New York State. Champlain had no idea how powerful the Iroquois were and what a bad idea it was make them your enemy. All

Sticks and Stones and Nasty Names

Iroquois means "real adders (snakes)" in the Abenaki language, so naturally the Iroquois didn't call themselves that. Europeans often made that mistake, calling people by the names that their enemies called them. For example, when the French met the Sioux people, they didn't realize that Sioux means "snakes in the grass." That's why the Sioux like to be called the Lakota, their own name for themselves. The Iroquois called themselves the Haudenosaunee, or People of the Longhouse. The Haudenosaunee were an alliance of five tribes: the Cayuga, the Mohawk, the Onondaga, the Oneida, and the Seneca.

Champlain knew was that the Huron and their Algonquin allies had lightweight birchbark canoes, while the Haudenosaunee used much chunkier dugouts. Champlain thought he had made a good deal in siding with the Hurons and their Algonquin allies. After all, the Algonquins showed the French a whole new area that no other Europeans had ever seen before — the Great Lakes. Eventually, the French would get their Native American guides to show them the Mississippi, the Native American name for that river. The French claimed not only all the lands around the Mississippi but also the great river sys-tem that flowed from the Ohio River. (Ohio is yet another Native American name.) Now, it's one thing to say, "Great, now all this belongs to France." It's another to actually *settle* a colony. Very few people were willing to leave France. Meanwhile, the English were on their way to America in big numbers. And the English came to stay.

Native Americans would soon find out it didn't matter much who sided with the Europeans.

These clothes are

so stinky I could jump in a vat of expired milk
and you still wouldn't be able to smell me.
Especially with a gas mask on! (Where did he
get that thing anyway? I guess there's NOTHING

these Native Americans can't get in exchange
for a pile of gold.)

But the colonists didn't have time to worry
about smelling so bad that even a dog would
faint. They had bigger fish to fry. Actually, they
didn't have ANY fish to fry. Otherwise, why
would they eat their own shoes??? I can understand *licking* a shoe if there was something tasty
stuck to the bottom of it . . . but *eating* the
whole shoe??? YECH!!! Although there is one
advantage, I guess. When you're finished eating,
you can use the shoelaces to floss your teeth.

Chapter 2

Yes, Virginia, There Is a Colony

When English toes first trod on America's beaches, they were wearing heavy boots. Some of the men and boys hitting the beaches also wore armor, but they couldn't have looked like much of a threat to Spain or France. Most of them later starved to death. England's first attempts to settle in North America were kind of puny. Still,

TIME LINE

1585–90
England loses two colonies on Roanoke Island

1607
Jamestown settled; Captain John Smith meets Pocahontas

1614
First tobacco crop shipped to England

42

from a tiny toehold in Virginia, English people eventually got a firm grip on the Atlantic seacoast. Virginians would turn out to have a huge impact on American history.

- They were the first colonists to actually make money off the land; they grew tobacco.

- They were the first to elect their own legislature.

- Virginians were the first to use African slaves.

- George Washington, a colonist from Virginia, would become the first president of the United States.

- Thomas Jefferson, another son of Virginia, would write the Declaration of Independence and became the third U.S. president.

The colonists brought us pigs, too. Magical animals! Bacon! Sausage! Ham! But does anyone ever mention pigs? NOOO! It's all Pilgrims, Puritans, and Pocahontas!

1616–18
Plague hits Native Americans from Florida to New England

1619
First African slaves in Virginia; first elected assembly

1644
Powhatan defeated

How Virginia Got Its Name

We don't have a state named Elizabeth (although this author thinks it would be a very good idea if we did). However, Virginia *is* named for England's Queen Elizabeth I. Confused? Well, Queen Elizabeth I was also known as the Virgin Queen because she never married, and "virgin" means someone who has never had sex. Queen Elizabeth I might have been a virgin, but that didn't mean she couldn't fall in love. And she did. Quite often. There is very little doubt that she was in love with Sir Walter Raleigh. Sir Walter wanted to go to America, but Queen Elizabeth was so fond of him that she refused to let him sail there himself. Still, Raleigh wanted to found a colony in America, so he paid for a group of men and boys to go the New World. He told them to name their colony Virginia, after his Virgin Queen.

Aaahh!
Come on!
All the other guys
get to go
to America!

You Wear Pretty Clothes

The men and boys sponsored by Sir Walter Raleigh landed on Roanoke Island off the coast of what is now North Carolina. They named the whole area Virginia. The Englishmen built a little fort — well, it was more like a cellar. They dug a hole in the ground and called it home. The Secotan people who were already living in the area kept calling the English *wingan-da-ca,* which meant "you're wearing pretty clothes." The Europeans wore armor, steel hats, and padded breeches, pants that went down to their knees. The Secotan people painted or tattooed beautiful designs on their bodies and wore necklaces and bracelets of shells, beads, and bones, but little clothing.

Things didn't go swimmingly for those first

The English saw things were going to be *very* different from now on.

English settlers in Virginia, maybe because they were wearing too many clothes for the climate. The Englishmen were kind of hoping to collect gold the way the Spaniards had in the New World. In other words, they were hoping to get other people to pick it up *for* them. Instead, the English picked up ticks and fleas and picked fights with the Secotans. When an English pirate, Sir Francis Drake, happened to sail by to see how they were doing, Sir Walter Raleigh's colonists begged him to get them out of there. They scrambled on board Drake's ships and went back to England.

A Colony Plays Hide-and-Seek

Sir Walter Raleigh decided to spend more of his money to send another group of colonists to live in Virginia. This time he thought it would be a better idea to send some women with the men. He hoped that having their families around would encourage the men to make their homes in the New World.

In 1587, 115 settlers sailed to Roanoke Island, including 15 married women, 2 single women, and 9 children. Two years later, they had all disappeared. No bodies were ever found. Nobody has solved the mystery of the lost colony at Roanoke.

Hey, James, Get a Town

After Queen Elizabeth died in 1603, England's new king, James I, liked the idea of having colonies in the New World, but he didn't want to pay for them. He gave royal grants to two groups of businessmen to pay for new colonies in Virginia. On May 13, 1607, 105 men and boys landed in Virginia on the Chesapeake Bay. They named the place Jamestown after their king. The colonists built a triangular fort made of pointed logs that were 11 feet tall. The fort was the size of about four football fields. It was the first permanent English town in America.

The Jamestown colonists lived in tents that entire first summer while they built their homes. The land where the colonists built was swampy, the drinking water was putrid, and bloodthirsty mosquitoes swarmed everywhere.

The colonists in Jamestown spent more time arguing about who should dig the wells and build the houses than they did digging or building. Since they hadn't brought enough beer to keep them alive,

They say English food is terrible. But I must say, as a mosquito, I love eating English!

Water, Water Everywhere and Not a Drop to Drink

European colonists didn't usually drink water because it so often made them sick. Mostly they drank beer, even for breakfast, because the alcohol in it killed some of the germs. Even children drank watered-down beer. Usually a brewery was one of the first things to be built in a settlement, after a church and a couple of homes.

they needed water. They didn't dig wells but just took water from the James River when the tide was out and the river wasn't too salty. The water made them sick. About half of the original Jamestown settlers were dead by the end of the first summer. By winter, there were fewer than 40 people left. The survivors put up the simplest houses they could, lit-

Mmmmmm! It's nutty!

James River Water

DRINK LIKE A COLONIST

tle huts with walls made of sticks and mud and thatched roofs. They were the kinds of huts that the poorest people in Europe had lived in for centuries. No fireplaces, just a hole in the roof. And they did almost no planting. They wanted to get the local Native Americans to give them food.

Meet the Powhatan

The English didn't realize it, but they had left crowded England and landed in one of the most crowded areas of what is now the United States. The Powhatan people who lived in Virginia called their home "the densely inhabited land."

The Powhatan leader was Wahunsonacock. (The English often just called him Powhatan.) Wahunsonacock had just completed an empire-building binge. He had started with six tribes whose rule he had inherited from his mother. By 1607, the year the English landed, he held power over 32 tribes and 15,000 people from Maryland to North Carolina.

Wahunsonacock already knew of Europeans from the Spaniards and French. The Jamestown settlers wanted him to accept the religion of the King of England. Wahunsonacock wasn't interested in their religion, but he was interested in English metal tools, copper pots, and blankets. Above all, he was interested in getting guns to use against other tribes who were his traditional enemies.

Almost as soon as trading began between the settlers and the Powhatan, violence broke out. Each side accused the other of stealing. Then the three ships sailed back to England for more supplies, and the colonists were on their own. They named Captain John Smith as their leader.

Captain John Smith: Swashbuckler Extraordinaire!

Artist's concept: a buckled Swash

If ever there was a man who had buckled many a swash, it was Captain John Smith. When John Smith sailed to Virginia, he was 27 years old, but already he had lived more lives than most cats. He had been captured and forced to be a princess's slave in Turkey. He was sold again, escaped, fought pirates in North Africa, and swashbuckled through Russia, Poland, and Germany. Then he landed in America. There, a Native American princess saved his life. Or *did* she?

Pocahontas Saves a Life — Maybe . . .

In December 1607, John Smith went exploring, hoping to trade with the Powhatan. Wahunsonacock's brother, Opechancanough, captured Smith and took him to Wahunsonacock. Smith probably felt good when he got to sit by the fire and share a feast. But then the party turned nasty. The Powhatan brought out two large stones and forced Smith's head on them. Warriors lifted their clubs as if to kill him. When John Smith first wrote about it, he didn't mention that a young girl threw herself over his body and pleaded for his life. But later, back in England, he penned his adventures again, and this time he wrote, "(B)eing ready with their clubs to beat out [my] brains, Pocahontas, the king's dearest daughter, got my head in her arms and laid

her own upon [mine] to save me from death."
Well, Captain John Smith had also claimed that
a Turkish princess saved his life. How many
princesses do most men get in their lives? Many
historians believe that Wahunsonacock was making Smith go through an initiation rite that
would make him feel that he owed Wahunsonacock his life. This was one way that tribes
created diplomatic ties among themselves.

When Smith got back to Jamestown, the
colonials were having a horrible time. New ships
of colonists had arrived, but a fire almost
destroyed the fort. One hundred and fifty men
had to share three huts. It was January and the
colonists were mostly starving, which is worse
than being "mostly hungry," but better than
being "mostly dead." Wahunsonacock sent
Pocahontas into Jamestown every few days with
gifts of deer meat and raccoon skins. She may
have been 10 or 11 years old then. The English
settlers wrote that Pocahontas did handstands in
their town. There is no proof of any romance
between her and John Smith.

In 1609, while Smith was sleeping on his
boat, a bag of gunpowder exploded, badly burning his leg. Because of his injury, he left for England, never to see Virginia again. Smith did
return to North America in 1614. He sailed north
to Maine and then south to Cape Cod and named
the whole area "New England."

Pocahontas: Cute but Bald

Several myths grew up around Pocahontas, most of them not true. Actually her real name was Matowaka, which can also be spelled Matoaka. Pocahontas was her nickname and meant "frisky" in the Powhatan language. Pocahontas is often depicted with her hair in pigtails, an unlikely hairdo. Most young Powhatan girls went around practically bald. Their hair was cut very short so it wouldn't attract bugs in the forest. Maybe the English should have copied this hairstyle — according to their journals they were lousy with head lice.

Head lice? And us roaches get the bad rap? How'd you like a case of head roaches?

In April 1613, Pocahontas was kidnapped by the English and forced to stay in Jamestown. She studied the Bible and changed her name to Rebecca. Perhaps it was in church that she met an Englishman, John Rolfe, whom she married in 1614. Two years later, she and her husband and their son went to England. Pocahontas got smallpox and died just as she was about to sail back to Virginia in 1617; she was probably 22 years old. But her son, Thomas, survived. He was educated in England and later returned to the colonies. His family became one of the wealthiest and most prominent in Virginia.

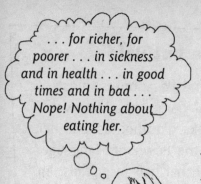

... *for richer, for poorer ... in sickness and in health ... in good times and in bad ... Nope! Nothing about eating her.*

Virginia's Own Hannibal, the Cannibal

John Smith got out of Virginia just in the nick of time. The winter of 1609 and 1610 became known as the "starving time." One colonist got so hungry that he killed his wife and ate "all parts saving her head." He was executed for doing that. No reports if anybody ate *his* body, but of the 500 people who had been alive when Smith left, only 60 were alive the next spring. Wahunsonacock decided to try to get rid of them all. He refused to sell the colonists any more food. His warriors surrounded the little fort at Jamestown so the English couldn't go out and hunt (and, of course, there were no pizza deliveries).

In May 1610, two English ships showed up in Virginia with supplies and settlers. These newcomers had gotten yellow fever while sailing from England, so they were already sick. When they took one look at the starving skin-and-bones survivors in Jamestown, everybody, new settlers and old, said, "Hey, this wasn't in the travel brochure." They jumped on the ships and headed for home. The Powhatan and Chief Wahunsonacock were happy to see them go.

Just then, 300 more new settlers sailed into Jamestown, led by Thomas West, Baron De La Warr. He turned everybody around and rebuilt Jamestown. The houses still had thatched roofs and dirt floors, but they were a little larger than the settlement's first huts. Wooden beams were placed in a frame, and the walls were filled in with a mix of twigs, straw, mud, and clay, which made them warmer in winter. Some chimneys were moved to the outside walls to keep things cooler in the summer. Eventually, some brick houses were built, and one of them was a tavern. Everybody went to the tavern. It was a place where people could gossip and have a smoke.

I'll bet those settlers belted out a rousing chorus of "99 Bottles of Beer on the Wall"!

At least they don't make us wear high heels.

Who Are You Calling a Puddinghead? Or Ma, This Corset's Killing Me!

Now that the settlers were here to stay, eventually more babies were born. Shortly after birth, babies were made to wear padded leather hats called "puddinghead caps" to protect the soft tops of their heads. Toddlers were sometimes fitted with a big pillow around their waists so that when they fell they wouldn't hurt themselves. Both boys and girls wore dresses until they were about six years old. The dress was a simple T-shaped tunic that was tied in the back. When they were about 16 to 18 months old, all children were fitted with a corsetlike article with bone stays that went from their hips to their rib cages. They even had to sleep in stays, but the sleep stays were a little more comfortable. This corset was supposed to make you sit up straight; girls would have to wear stays all their lives. And was that uncomfortable? Of corset it was!

Tobacco: The Weed
That Changed History

John Rolfe was one of the settlers who came to Jamestown with Baron De La Warr in 1610. (Four years later, he fell in love with and married Pocahontas.) Rolfe loved to smoke, and he had brought some tobacco seeds from the West Indies with him. Rolfe planted his seeds in Virginia soil. Tobacco was going to make Rolfe and lots of the other Virginia colonists rich.

In 1614, John Rolfe shipped about 100 pounds of tobacco to England and got a good price for it. A dozen years later, Virginia planters were shipping 500,000 pounds of tobacco a year to England. Tobacco is a big plant. Its lower leaves are as long as two feet. It needs a lot of room to grow. Suddenly, the English colonists wanted to grab all the land they could get. The investors back in England tried to get more

Grasshoppers of the tobacco patch thought they were so much cooler than other grasshoppers.

people to come to Virginia. Anyone who could pay for a voyage was promised 50 acres of land. Tobacco became like gold.

Indentured Servants:
How About Jail if You Don't Pay
Your Credit Card Bill?

It takes a lot of hard work and a lot of skill to grow tobacco. The plants have to be taken care of almost year-round. It was hard to find people to work the fields. In the beginning, most of the people working Virginia's tobacco fields were indentured servants. "Indentured" meant you worked for seven years with no pay, but after that you were free. So who would want to work for seven years for no pay? Poor people!

It was tough being poor in England. England was going through enormous changes, switching from a country where most people farmed to a country where a few people were making huge amounts of money from trade and manufacturing. Thousands of people were being thrown off the farms and wandering through the cities, begging and looking for work.

In England, you could be put in jail if you didn't pay your

Just as Mr. Thavershim finished his ham sandwich, he realized he'd left his wallet in his other pants.

debts. One way out of debt was to go to the colonies as an indentured servant. Your voyage was paid for, but indentured servants were packed into ships like slaves. If the ship ran out of food, the servants starved. Indentured servants could be bought and sold like slaves. They could be whipped for talking back to their masters.

The Doggy and the Kids Go 'Round and 'Round

Man! I hope no other dogs see this.

Dogs and kids helped out in the kitchen. Usually, a child or servant was given the job of turning the spit so that the meat would cook evenly. Sometimes a dog was trained to run on a wheel that turned the spit. Dogs were also sometimes trained to churn butter by putting them on a kind of treadmill that was connected to a butter churn.

The early tobacco farms were not the lush life of plantation living. The average planter lived in an unpainted wooden shack about the size of a two-car garage. A single room served as the family's kitchen, dining area, and workroom. Food was mostly a gruel of ground corn. Women helped out in the fields, and then they were responsible for all the cooking, a very dangerous job. A full 25 percent of colonial women died when their clothes caught on fire while they were cooking.

African Slaves: The Awful Solution

From the colonial planter's point of view, the problem with indentured servants was that after seven years they had to be paid wages and they could leave. The planters began to look around for people who would work the tobacco fields and who could never leave. They tried to make slaves of the Native Americans they met. But the Native Americans kept fighting back or slipping away into the woods.

In 1619, a ship from Holland sailed into Jamestown, carrying slaves from the West Indies. The Dutch sold the English 20 "negars" from the West Indies, probably descendants of Africans brought to the West Indies as slaves. These were the first people of African descent to be enslaved in what is now the United States.

Most Africans who came to the United States between 1600 and 1670 didn't come directly from Africa. Most had first lived in the West Indies. They usually spoke one or more European languages as well as their original language from Africa. Some of them had already converted to Christianity. Virginia passed a law that said that any Africans who were Christian before they came to Virginia had the right to work for their freedom. A few Africans were able to earn their freedom in the same way that white indentured servants could. African slavery didn't take hold immediately in Virginia. It was too expensive for most planters, and the death rate of slaves was high. By 1650, there were only 405 Africans in Virginia and about 18,000 whites.

Right to Vote: Not So Fast if You're Black, Female, or a Servant

England was going through a lot of turmoil back home. It had all those fights about religion and wars with Spain, France, and Holland. It didn't really have time to worry too much about how to rule the colonies. The English colonies developed in a topsy-turvy way, making up rules as they went along.

In the beginning, the main purpose of Virginia was for the colonists there to make money for their investors back home in England. (Another reason was that the English king wanted to keep up with Spain and France.) Now, with the successful tobacco crops, the investors were actually getting some money back.

But 3,000 miles and a huge ocean lay between the investors and the folks actually living in Virginia. The investors appointed a colonial governor who was responsible to them and to the king. The governor made the rules for the colonists and decided how much tax they should pay. But it was hard for the governor to get anybody to actually obey the rules and pay the taxes.

**Colonial governing techniques
prior to granting self-rule**

The investors in England decided that they could get more people to go to Virginia if they let the colonists have some say in writing the rules for the colony. In 1619, they allowed each of the little Virginia settlements up and down the James River to elect an assembly called the

House of Burgesses. No women, servants, or slaves could vote. Oh, sure, they could do all the work and burn themselves while cooking dinner, but they couldn't vote.

The first time the House of Burgesses met, it made a rule that all planters had to grow food as well as tobacco. It made other rules about how much food would be kept in the storehouse. In other words, the English colonists in Virginia now had some control over how they would live.

The Powhatan Try
to Take Back
Their Land

White male English colonists in Virginia had an actual say in the way they were governed. They also had a crop that made them money and some had slaves to work the land. Things were looking up for the English settlers. But for the Powhatan, the news was all bad. The worst thing that happened to them was an epidemic of European diseases that swept through their people around 1617 to 1618. One of the people to die was Wahunsonocock. Opechancanough, Wahunsonacock's brother, then became chief. Opechancanough considered it his duty to get rid of the English. In 1622, he almost succeeded. Powhatan warriors slaughtered more than 347

What a depressing page! I can't joke about a page like this. I'm sorry . . . give me a minute . . . keep reading, I'll catch up.

English women, men, and children, most of them on little farms outside Jamestown. The new English governor, Francis Wyatt, called for a peace conference. When Opechancanough and his warriors showed up, Governor Wyatt fed them poison. Opechancanough escaped, but 200 of his warriors died.

By 1644, Opechancanough was almost 100 years old and blind, but he led a final fight against the English. He had to be carried to the battle on a litter. He was captured. The new governor, William Berkeley, ordered that Opechancanough be treated kindly, knowing that he was very near death. But a guard shot him in the back and killed him. After that, the once-powerful Powhatan were never able to seriously threaten the English in Virginia.

 **Jamestown Settlement Plantation** and **Powhatan Village, Virginia.** The **Colonial National Historical Park** is more than 9,327 acres in Tidewater, Virginia. Both the Jamestown fort and a Powhatan village have been re-created, and costumed guides will show you around. Inside the re-created fort, you can try on English armor and see where Pocahontas probably did handstands.

No wonder

the English didn't fit in right away. Who goes to the beach dressed in a full suit of armor? Just look at all these people having fun in the sun and I can't do any of it. I can't play volleyball; I can't play Frisbee; and I certainly can't go swimming. I'd sink like a rock! Not to mention, I'm so hot I feel like I'm standing in an oven. I'd give anything for a tall, cool glass of water, but all they have around here is beer . . . warm beer! YECH! I'd rather drink a glass of sand! And do you want to know the worst thing about this crazy get-up? I've been on a diet for three months just to get in shape for bikini season! Do you know how hard it is for a cockroach to cut back on eating? It's like asking a lion not to roar or asking a skunk not to stink. It's just not natural! And now I can't show off my body!!! This is the worst trip to the beach I've ever had. Next year, remind me to pack a swimsuit and leave this steel suit home.

Chapter 3
New England Tries to Be Pure

A pilgrim is anybody who takes a trip for religious reasons. The first English settlers in New England didn't call themselves Pilgrims, but that's what they eventually became known as. They left England because they wanted to separate from the King's Church, and he would not let them. They called themselves "Saints." Pilgrims are often pictured wearing only black

TIME LINE

1620
Mayflower Compact; Saints settle Plymouth

1630
Puritans start coming in large numbers to Massachusetts

1635–36
Smallpox epidemic kills Native Americans; Roger Williams starts Rhode Island

68

The rarely depicted tie-dye Pilgrims

with tall black hats, but actually they didn't wear black all that much. They liked to dye their clothes as brightly as they could.

The *Mayflower:* It Didn't Smell Sweet

In 1620, a ship called the *Mayflower* landed at what is now Massachusetts. There were no flowers on the ship, only cold, wet, miserable kids, parents, and sailors. They were a young crowd: 69 adults and 33 kids and teenagers. The *Mayflower* had sailed in the middle of winter. It took 66 days to reach America, twice as long as it took Columbus. During the trip, everybody ate

1675–76	1684	1692
King Philip's War	Massachusetts becomes royal colony	Salem witch trials

moldy cheese and sea biscuits that were as hard as rocks and full of maggots. They often liked to eat at night in the dark so they didn't have to look at the bugs. They almost ran out of beer, which everybody drank, even the children. Nobody took a bath or washed clothes during the two-month trip. They all probably stank.

Only about 41 of the *Mayflower*'s passengers were Saints who wanted to go to America so they could start a separate church and worship as they chose. The Saints called the rest of the passengers on the *Mayflower* "Strangers." The Strangers were not coming to North America for religious reasons. They were coming either because they wanted adventure or because life was so miserable for them in England.

The Mayflower Compact
(Not a Makeup Brand)

The Strangers didn't necessarily want to follow the religious rules of the Saints. They figured that when they hit land, they'd go their own way. Around Nantucket, off the coast of Massachusetts, the Saints got everybody to agree to what they called the Mayflower Compact. This was the first set of rules on how to live in America written by settlers themselves (actually just the male settlers since the women weren't invited to sign the Compact). They agreed to work together for *equal* laws and for the good of everybody.

On November 11, 1620, the *Mayflower* dropped anchor off Cape Cod. Everybody spent the Sabbath (Sunday) on board, but on Monday, the women went ashore to wash clothes. Monday became the day to wash clothes for hundreds of years in New England.

The colonists on the *Mayflower* spent nearly a month looking for a good place to build their homes. Just a little north of Cape Cod, they came to a place with a pretty brook bubbling down a hill and fields already cleared for planting. The colonists knew that Native Americans had cleared this land for corn, but the place looked deserted. They decided this was a great spot; Plymouth, Massachusetts, would become their home.

Family Life: What to Call the New Baby

The only baby born on the *Mayflower* was named Oceanus Hopkins because he had been born at sea. Children were often named for something that happened at the moment of their birth. You could be named Fathergone if your father was dead or had gone missing. Sometimes you were given a name like Comfort, Deliverance, Peace, Hope, Patience, Charity, Faith, or Love in the hope that you would live up to it. Then there were odder names like Waitstill, Preserved, and Hopestill. One colonial New England family had kids named Return, Believe, and Tremble. There's no record of any babies named Uglyface or Big Nose.

Mr. Dad's-a-Bad-Barber, I'd like you to meet Miss Mom-Loves-to-Cook.

Misery

All through the winter of 1620–21, the group from the *Mayflower* lived aboard the ship while they started to build homes on land. In that cold, wet winter, cramped in the hold of the *Mayflower,* they started dying like flies.

Every day, another English child, woman, or man died. In the middle of the night, the survivors would sneak down the gangplank of the *Mayflower* and secretly bury their dead on the hill. Although they hadn't really seen any Native Americans, the colonists knew they were there. They were afraid that if the Native Americans saw how many colonists were dying, they would attack the survivors.

At the top of the hill, the colonists built a common house made of mud and wood. They moved their gunpowder and cannons into it, but chimney sparks caused the thatched roof to catch fire twice. In February, rain melted the mud-daubed walls of the few structures the settlers had managed to build. All in all, it was a miserable first winter.

Welcome, Englishmen!

On March 16, 1621, the door to the common house opened, and a tall stranger entered. "Welcome, Englishmen," he said. "Me Samoset."

Thatched Roofs

Thatch is made of the stalks of tall plants like reeds. It can take more than a million stalks to make a roof, but if a thatched roof doesn't catch fire, it lasts for more than 20 years before it has to be replaced. Thatched roofs were common in England, and they are still used there for some country homes and taverns.

Balding Englishmen found that "thatched heads" were not only fashionable, but kept them dry!

According to some historians he may have also said, "Me want beer." Samoset was an Abenaki from Maine who had learned English when an English fishing vessel had carried him south to Cape Cod.

Samoset spent the night at the home of Stephen Hopkins, who stayed up the whole time watching him. In the morning, Samoset was given a knife, a bracelet, and a ring as gifts. He promised the settlers he would come back with someone who spoke even better English. A few days later Samoset came back with a man named Tisquantum, often called Squanto.

At the first meeting that Tisquantum arranged between the settlers and the Wampanoag, Chief Massasoit arrived at the settlement with his face painted purple. His warriors had painted their faces black, red, yellow, and white. Governor John Carver greeted him, followed by a drummer and a trumpet player. It wasn't quite as impressive as painted warriors, but it was a start. The governor kissed Massasoit's hand, and they sat in an unfinished house on a green rug and brightly colored cushions. Tisquantum translated.

Massasoit was mostly interested in getting the English to side with him against his traditional enemies, the Narraganset. The English were mostly interested in just getting help surviving. They agreed to what is called a mutual alliance treaty. That basically means, "I'll watch your back, if you watch mine." Massasoit agreed to trade food for English goods and to let

If we're in a fight, you'll help us, right?

Oh, you betcha!

I think the English got the best of this deal.

Tisquantum stay with them. The English were desperate for food. Half of them were dead and the other half were nearly starving.

Fish Heads and Low Ceilings

That first spring, Tisquantum taught the colonists how to plant corn, beans, squashes, and "pompions," a.k.a. pumpkins, in the same mound. It's a great system. The corn grows tall at the top; the beans use the corn as a pole, and the squash or pompions cover the ground around the mound and keep weeds from growing. In every mound, Tisquauntum told the English to throw a few herring heads in with the seeds. Fish are great fertilizer. He also taught them how to eat lobster.

You're soooo slimy, and you smell extra fishy! I bet you'd make great fertilizer!

Fish love talk

During the summer, the colonists were able to build real homes for themselves. They built one-room houses with ceilings so low that anybody more than five feet tall bumped their heads. The little houses always smelled of smoke because, as in Virginia, the fire had to be constantly kept lit. Once the colonists started to eat a little better, life got a lot jollier — but never on a Sunday.

Sunday worship services were long and dedicated to studying and reading the Bible. No work could be done. People couldn't even cook or make their beds. But the settlers in Plymouth were not against having a good time. They liked to wear clothes as bright and colorful as they could make them. And they enjoyed music and games, though not on Christmas. The Saints would not allow anybody to celebrate Christmas because the exact day of Jesus Christ's birth wasn't mentioned in the Bible. They felt that feasting or taking a day off from work was not the way to show that you were serious about God.

Thanksgiving: Turkeys? Maybe

The very first fall after the Plymouth settlers landed they decided to have a big party to celebrate the fact that they had survived and that there was something to eat. It's because of that party that we now have Thanksgiving. Here's what we know about that Thanksgiving of 1621 in Plymouth:

• It probably happened in early October 1621, because that's when the harvest would have been.

- Twice as many Wampanoag as English came to the party. Massasoit brought 90 warriors, apparently quite a few more than the colonists were planning for. Massasoit was the perfect guest, though. He immediately sent his warriors out to bring back five deer.

- They definitely ate those deer and a lot of duck and geese. What about the turkey? Well, there were wild turkeys around, but they were very hard to catch, and nobody knows if they were eaten at that first feast. The feast almost certainly included venison, ducks, geese, boiled lobster, corn stew, and eels. (Yes, eels!)

**The thoughts of woodland creatures
on that first Thanksgiving**

- Nobody sat at tables. There were too many people so they had to eat outdoors. Think of a big picnic with lots to eat and drink and people eating and sleeping on the ground and then waking up to do more partying. Party on!

- The settlers said that they celebrated with exercising of arms! Nope, not gym class. Think more of shooting guns into the air for the fun of it and marching in drills. There might have been target practice and contests with bows and arrows, so that Massasoit and the Wampanoag could show off how good they were.

Fortunately, we eventually did away with the guns, the bows, and the eels. Yech! Definitely get rid of the eels!

For Native Americans, Little to Be Thankful For

After that first Thanksgiving, Tisquantum began acting very suspiciously. Massasoit sent a more trusted adviser, Hobbamock, and his family to live near the English at Plymouth and act as an ambassador. Massasoit and the settlers at Plymouth kept an uneasy peace for nearly 40 years until Massasoit died.

During those years, more and more English people came to New England, and it became harder and harder to keep the peace. At first, the English tried to be careful and buy land from the Native Americans. They opened schools for Native Americans. Just like the colonists in Virginia, the English kept hoping that the Indians would accept their ways and become like them and not mind that they were taking their land.

From 1635 to 1636, a smallpox epidemic killed tens of thousands of Native Americans in the Connecticut River Valley. Most of the English thought of the smallpox epidemic as an act of God, emptying the land so that they could move in.

Connecticut and New Hampshire: Two New Cranky Colonies

English people moved into Connecticut in 1636 and New Hampshire in 1638, but in the beginning neither was a separate colony. Each place had many squabbles with its neighbors, particularly Massachusetts, which everybody considered very bossy. After the monarchy was restored in England, both Connecticut and New Hampshire appealed to get their own charters so that they could be separate from Massachusetts. In 1662, Connecticut got its own charter, and in 1680, New Hampshire got one, too. Massachusetts took back New Hampshire in 1690, but the New Hampshire people were a feisty lot and they got their charter back in 1692.

But, baby! We belong together!

State Divorce Court

Talk to the hand.

MASS.

N.H.

Pequot War

In 1636, a white man was found killed, floating in his boat on water that belonged to the Pequot. Although the Plymouth settlers knew he was a wild man and weren't completely sure how he died, they felt they had to punish the Pequot. The Pequot hoped Massasoit's Wampanoag and the Narraganset would join them in a fight against the English. But Massasoit decided to stick to the treaty he had signed with the settlers at Plymouth. Hoping to get more guns, the Narraganset actually helped the English attack a Pequot stronghold at what is now Mystic, Connecticut. The Pequot were surprised and their village burned, roasting the inhabitants. Those who tried to escape were slaughtered, even the children. The few Pequot who survived were

The Mashantucket Pequot Museum cost about $193 million dollars to build and goes way beyond just the history of the Pequot. You can use computer interactive studies to see how Native Americans lived in the Northeast from the Ice Age to the arrival of the Europeans.

sold into slavery. Their tribe was nearly wiped out. But the few who survived remembered, and in the 1990s, they insisted on their rights as a nation and got back a tiny piece of land in Connecticut. There they built one of the largest casinos in the world and a museum.

King Philip's War: Bloodiest in Colonial History

Massasoit died in 1660 when he was about 80 years old. When he died, some of the first settlers from Plymouth came to his burial to show their respect. Then Massasoit's elder son died, after being forced to come to Plymouth when he was sick. His younger son, Metacom, who was known by the English name Philip, took over as chief of the Wampanoag. Metacom might have had an English name, and he might have sometimes dressed in English clothes, but he believed the English were the worst enemy the Wampanoag had ever had. He began quietly trying to make alliances with other tribes, but most refused, just as his father had refused to help the Pequot.

In 1675, an English farmer killed a Wampanoag. Metacom went to the English courts in Plymouth, but they refused to do anything about it. To Metacom, that meant war. Metacom had grown up around the English and their guns and he knew how to use them. The war went on for two years. At first, the fighting all went in favor of the Wampanoag; 600 English men, women, and children lost their lives.

Gradually, all the colonists of the Northeast, even ones from as far away as Maine and New Hampshire, came together to fight. Some historians say this was the war that turned the English settlers into Americans, because now they were fighting together. The colonists caught Metacom in a trap and shot him. The Plymouth settlers, in order to celebrate their victory and teach the other tribes a lesson, chopped off Metacom's head and took it back to the Plymouth. They stuck it on a stake. By the end of the war, 3,000 Wampanoag were dead. This war became known as King Philip's War and by the percentage of the population that was killed, it was the bloodiest in American history. Metacom's head stayed on display in Plymouth, shriveling and drying up, for 25 years. Some say that the street corner where it was impaled is still haunted.

Plimoth Plantation has been re-created right outside of the original Plymouth, Massachusetts. (Note: If you're a lousy speller, the 17th century would have been for you. Most people just guessed about how to spell things.)

Guides play roles of the original settlers (although they draw the line at actually dying of starvation). Descendants of the Wampanoag re-create how **Hobbamock** and his family lived. In the town of

Plymouth, you can board a replica of the *Mayflower* and see **Plymouth Rock.** Some people videotape it, but it really isn't going anywhere. A statue of Massasoit overlooks Plymouth Harbor. In 1970, Thanksgiving was declared a **National Day of Mourning** by Native Americans, and Plymouth was chosen as the place to observe it.

The English Keep Coming

In the 20 years between 1620 and 1640, the number of English settlers in New England jumped from just a few hundred to almost 14,000. At the time, England was rocked by religious battles between a religious group called the Puritans and the Church of England. The Puritans wanted to purify the English church. They called the King's church a "puddle of corruption." King Charles I did not like his church being called a puddle. What king would? He tried killing a few Puritans or putting them in jail, but their numbers kept growing.

The king and his ministers then tried to get rid of the Puritans by letting them go to America. Soon, the fight between the Puritans and the supporters

For a while there, it seemed like English settlers were popping up like weeds.

of King Charles I started a civil war in England. Charles I got his head chopped off in 1649. All that turmoil in England meant that a lot of people wanted to come to America (even though when a head got chopped off in America, there was a tendency to keep it around for 25 years).

Puritan Ideals

Like the Saints, the Puritans wanted to build a world in which people would be as perfect as they could be and live life according to the laws of the Bible. Anybody who didn't follow their Puritan laws or believe in their religion was not welcome. Quakers (members of the Society of Friends) could have their ears cut off and have the letter H for heretic burned into their hands. They could be hanged. Disagree with the Puritans and you would be thrown out of the colony or even killed. The Puritans planted their idea about a righteous and religious life in the rocky New

Freedom of religion is all-important! People should worship as they think fit (unless you think differently, then we may have to kill you).

England soil, and like the Virginia settlers, they ended up having a huge effect on how many Americans came to think of themselves.

- The Puritans believed in being able to read the Bible for themselves. That meant that education was important and that the public should pay for it.

- They believed that hard work is important and that everything should be done in moderation, for example, not too much partying or dancing.

- Everybody was supposed to live in town and go out into the fields to farm. Today, many towns all over America are still built around a town square with the houses close together.

- Puritans believed that everyone in town, *if* they went to church, should have a say in how the town was run. Even though this idea of government included only people who went to church, it was very different from a king or queen making all the laws.

- All the fights and killing over religion in Puritan New England caused some New Englanders to decide that government should stay out of religion altogether. Some Puritans broke away from Massachusetts and founded colonies where people were free to worship however they wanted.

Puritan Boston, a City on the Hill

In 1630, John Winthrop brought 11 ships full of English Puritans to settle in Boston. He said it would be "as a city upon a hill, the eyes of all people are upon us." Winthrop and his followers thought they could model how all people should live. The Puritans really did want everyone to lead a pure, religious life, and they felt that the best way to do that was to live close together in a community so they could keep track of one another. Since religion was so important, the first building to go up was almost always the Puritan church, called a meetinghouse. The first meetinghouses were plain wood, usually without steeples. The benches were hardwood with no cushions.

The meetinghouse was the center of Puritan life, and it was often decorated in strange ways. Rewards were paid if you killed a wolf, and in order to prove that you killed one, you'd bring the wolf's head to the meetinghouse and pin it to the wall.

The Puritans helped one another build their houses, which were usually made of wooden boards, though later some were built of brick. Almost every house had a kitchen garden, and most people kept a cow or pig. Window glass had to be imported from England, and it was expensive. Besides, New England's cold winters made most colonists want very small windows.

Washing Windows with Pee

Colonial housewives sometimes washed the windows with rags dipped in pee. They didn't have any ammonia, and pee worked pretty well. Actually, fresh pee is very clean. (Note to kids: Do not try this at home, or you'll get the author in trouble!) Speaking of pee, nobody had to worry about wetting their underpants. Nobody wore underpants. Everyone — girls, boys, men, and women — wore a long shirt called a shift that he or she slept in and wore all day. People pulled their other clothes on over their shifts. When women needed to pee, they could just lift their skirts. Most people peed outdoors. Sometimes there were outhouses.

How many books are you going to read with phrases like "speaking of pee"?

AMERICA's HORRIBLE HISTORIES

School Days

One of the first things the Puritans did was to build schools. Education was so important to the Puritans that they made a law that any town with 50 or more people had to pay for a school-teacher. In 1635, they started Boston High and Latin Schools (these names are still in use today.) In 1636, Harvard College was founded. Students sometimes paid for their tuition in wampum, the belts of shells that Native Americans used to trade. Wampum was about the only form of money the early Puritans had. In order to make a little extra money on the side, one of the first Harvard headmasters bought meat that was rotten and charged the college for good meat.

Unlike most Europeans at the time, the Puritans believed that even girls should be taught to read the Bible. Although no girls were allowed in Harvard College, Puritan girls sometimes did go to school. Women became important in the churches of New England. In fact, in many churches, they outnumbered the men.

Boston Common: Cows and Gallows

Most houses in Boston were built around the common, a 50-acre grass field where the militia trained and cows and other animals roamed. It was the place to go for public entertainment, like watching someone get hanged, whipped, put in the stocks or on a dunking stool. The Puritans, like most other Europeans, believed that punishment should be carried out in public to teach everyone a lesson. And these punishments often turned into fairs with hawkers selling food to eat. Great fun for everyone except the person being punished and the ones who loved them.

Dunking stools were used on women who

No Falling Asleep in Church

Attending sermons in the meetinghouse was compulsory for Puritans, kind of like assemblies in school. Sermons could last for five or six hours, and you had to stay awake. Someone walked up and down the aisles, carrying a stick with a knob on one end and a dangling foxtail on the other. Tickling their noses with the foxtails usually woke up sleeping adults, but sleeping children — particularly boys — would get whacked on the side of their heads with the knob. So, generally, it was a good idea to sneak in a nap *before* the sermon.

**After hours of preaching,
some early Puritans had to revert
to the tag-team method.**

insulted somebody or were suspected of being witches. The woman was tied to a seat at the end of a long lever and dunked in the water again and again for 30 seconds at a time until she begged for mercy or said she was sorry. Sometimes, the woman drowned.

Roger Williams: A Wild and Crazy Guy

Roger Williams started out as a Puritan preacher in Boston but was run out of town. Williams was the Puritan version of a wild and crazy guy. How wild and crazy was Roger Williams?

- He believed that killing anybody in the name of Christianity, whether for cursing God or being a Quaker, was wrong.

- He believed that people should look to their own conscience to decide what was right.

- He believed that the land really belonged to the Native Americans.

For all those beliefs, Roger Williams was kicked out of Massachusetts in 1636. Rather than go back to England, he fled south. The only reason he survived was that the Wampanoag and Narraganset tribes helped him. Williams bought land from the Narraganset and started a colony that he called Providence, a word that means God caring for the universe. Providence would become the capital of Rhode Island. Roger Williams decided that everyone in Providence should be free to worship, even Catholics, Quakers, and Jews. He would even allow people who didn't believe in God into his colony.

Anne Hutchinson: Holy Rebel

In 1638, just two years after Roger Williams fled to Rhode Island, Anne Hutchinson was also kicked out of Boston. In Boston, Hutchinson had held prayer sessions in her home that encouraged people to speak to God for themselves. The

Sticky Stocks

The stocks were a pair of boards with holes for the ankles and hands and a seat made from the sharpened edge of a board. There was also a device called the pillory. People put in pillories had their heads and hands stuck in the holes between two boards, and no seat, so they had to stand. Both the stocks and the pillory were extremely uncomfortable. A crowd could come around and throw rotten food at you if you were in the stocks or pillory. Then ants and other insects would find that goo on your face very tasty. People sentenced to these punishments said the insects were the biggest problem because they couldn't shoo them away.

I'm a roach.
I need to crawl around!
Help!
There's a bug
on me!

Sometimes a loved one was allowed to wipe the face of the person in the stocks or pillory. One sea captain was put in the stocks for a day for kissing his wife on Sunday in public. (He hadn't seen her in three years.)

Puritan ministers felt that people should listen to their sermons, not to the words of a woman. They told Hutchinson she was "stepping out of her place." When her prayer sessions got even more popular than their sermons, Hutchinson was accused of heresy and was banished. She, her family, and her loyal followers moved to Rhode Island to be with Roger Williams. After her husband died, Hutchinson moved to New York State, where she and her daughters were killed in a Native American raid in 1643. John Winthrop, the Puritan leader, said that this was God's punishment.

Thinking about what had happened to him and to Anne Hutchinson, Roger Williams wrote, "Forced worship stinks in God's nostrils." He decided it would be better if the government did not follow any one religion, and he made that the law in Rhode Island.

Looking to Get Rich in New England

As more and more English people moved into New England, dozens of towns sprang up throughout the countryside. Soon there would be more than 130 different towns in the region. Many of the people in these towns were more interested in finding ways to make a living than they were in religion.

As people became richer they wanted lots of things that riches could buy. One merchant in Boston built himself a mansion with 11 rooms, and he was said to have imported furniture from England that was worth more than 7,000 British pounds sterling, a fortune in those days.

The Africans in New England and the Slave Trade

One way to show off your new riches was to own a slave. In 1687, a visitor to Boston said, "There is not a house in Boston, however small may be its name that has not one or two African servants." This visitor must have visited only wealthy homes. The truth was that most Bostonians, in fact most New Englanders did not own slaves. In 1715, there were about 4,000 slaves out of a total population of about 160,000.

Although most New Englanders didn't own slaves, many were making money through slavery. Before the 1660s, most slave traders were Spanish, Portuguese, or Dutch. But English sailors soon got into the act. For a while, only the Royal African Company was allowed to sell slaves. In 1698, the English parliament ended the Royal African Company's monopoly. Now anybody with enough money to hire a ship could get into the slave trade. Good news for colonists — bad news for Africans. In New England, one of the quickest ways to get rich was to get into the slave trade. Ships would leave Boston or Newport filled with timber, cod, and furs. In England, they'd pick up manufactured goods and guns and sail to Africa. In Africa, they'd trade the goods and guns for slaves.

Most of the slavers involved in the slave

trade didn't sell their slaves in North America. Most African slaves were shipped either to the West Indies or to South and Central America. In the 1700s, American colonists made as much money from transporting slaves as they did growing any crops.

Puritans: A Little Less Pure

More and more people moved into New England looking to get rich, and not just from the slave trade. In Saugus, just north of Boston, the Puritans built the first ironworks in America. More shops were built in Boston and other towns. As time went by, New Englanders became interested in living their lives without the clergy telling them what was right and what was wrong.

The Puritans had lost control in England, too. After Charles I was beheaded in 1649, the Puritans ruled England for 11 years. But then, in 1660, the English got tired of them. The people loyal to Charles's son, Charles II, defeated the Puritans and England has had a king or queen ever since.

When Charles II died, the new king, James II, sent a royal governor to New England, to make the colonists behave and pay taxes. The New Englanders didn't like that. The governor, Edmund Andros, was seized by an angry mob. Some sources say he escaped wearing a woman's dress. Still, Andros was eventually imprisoned and sent home to England.

All in all, toward the turn of the 17th century, the Puritans felt that their ideals were slipping. Some historians believe that it was precisely because they felt their power slipping away that the Puritans came down so hard on a group of people accused of witchcraft in Salem, Massachusetts.

Salem had been one of the first towns to be settled by Puritans. By 1692, it had grown to almost 2,000 people, with many people living on farms a little way from town. These people became used to going their own way, and they didn't always agree with the new Puritan minister in town. Big mistake.

Salem's Witch's Brew

In 1692, nine young girls in Salem, including the minister's daughters, claimed that witches were possessing them. One of the women they accused was a slave, Tituba, who was either African-American or perhaps a native of the West Indies. Tituba was forced to make a cake out of rye meal mixed with the pee from two of the girls and feed it to a dog. If the dog acted strangely, that was supposed to be proof that Tituba had bewitched the girls. Apparently, the dog didn't act in any way that was sure proof, but

soon the girls were acting weirder and weirder. Eventually, Tituba confessed to being a witch, and her life was spared.

But some of the other women whom the girls accused were not so lucky. Sarah Goode was hanged by her neck until dead. Her last words to the judge were, "I am no more a witch than you are a wizard, and if you take away my life, God will give you blood to drink." Soon, all sorts of adults got into the act. The jails became packed with more than 100 women and men suspected by their neighbors of being witches. A four-year-old child was even jailed.

Boston and **Salem, Massachusetts.** The Boston Common has a statue to Anne Hutchinson and you can see Frog Pond where the dunkings took place. The **Boston National Historical Park** links a number of different colonial and revolutionary sites. Salem has many activities to teach about the witch trials. You can visit the **Salem Wax Museum** and the **Salem Witch Museum.** There is a memorial art exhibit to the victims of the witch trials in one of the graveyards and, as you might expect, many special events take place on Halloween.

Imagine how much trouble you'd be in if you had visited Salem during the witch trials.

Whassup?

Many people in Salem and in Boston began worrying that this whole witchcraft thing was getting out of hand. The trials were suspended. In 1693, the governor of Massachusetts pardoned the remaining accused. But by that time, 19 people had died by hanging, and one had died by being crushed to death. In 1697, the Massachusetts court asked for a day of forgiveness for the way they had acted during the trials, and one of the judges, Samuel Sewall, publicly confessed his feelings of guilt. No one was ever tried for being a witch in Massachusetts again.

Hello, my little

pretties! You'll have to excuse my pet dog.
I know it looks like he's just sipping from his
favorite watering hole, but actually my pup
is feeling a little sick ever since he had to
eat a cake made out of pee. There must be

better ways of telling if a person's a witch!

First of all, if you see someone wearing a funny hat (like the one I'm wearing) and if that someone's got a black cape (like the one I've got) and is riding around on a broom (like this broom in my hand), *then* you're talking witch. Hey! That must mean I'm a witch! Oh, boy! I think the first thing I'll do is cast a spell on all humans to make them drop a big piece of food on the ground every time they eat. That's what I call "using my powers for good."

Chapter 4
Rowdy, Muddled Middle Colonies

How about a place where Quakers don't have to worry about being hanged? How about a town where one in every four buildings is a tavern where people could catch up on the latest gossip? Or a place where Ben Franklin could tell you jokes? If that kind of place appeals to you, then you would most likely have ended up in what became known as the middle colonies:

TIME LINE

1626
Dutch get
New Amsterdam

1632
Catholics get
Maryland

1638
Swedes get
New Jersey

104

New York, New Jersey, Pennsylvania, Delaware, and Maryland.

They were called the "middle colonies" because they were in the middle, between New England and the southern colonies. The middle colonies were a mix of new immigrants from Holland, Sweden, Germany, France, and Africa. All these different nationalities rubbing up against one another made for a colorful and sometimes muddled history. It meant that not one religious group could dominate. Starting with New York, almost by default, all of these colonies began a tradition of religious tolerance.

The Big Apple Didn't Start Out Big

During the Colonial Era, the Dutch were a power to be reckoned with. They had fast ships and were setting up bits and pieces of an empire all over the world. The Dutch managed to escape the religious wars that were roiling throughout Europe. In Holland, Protestants, Catholics, and

1664	1706	1712 & 1741
English take over New York	Benjamin Franklin born	Slave uprisings in New York

**The first huts on the
island of Manhattan**

Jews lived together. They would do that in the
New World, too.

In 1609, the Dutch paid an English sailor,
Henry Hudson, to go to the New World for them.
Hudson sailed into an amazing harbor where
today the Statue of Liberty stands. By 1626, the
Dutch had built two dozen tree-bark huts on an
island called Manhattan, named after the
Manhattes people who lived there. The Dutch
named their town New Amsterdam (now New
York City) after their home in Holland. On the
southern tip of Manhattan where most of the
Dutch lived, they built canals because that's
what they had in Holland. In the winter, the
canals would freeze and the people skated
around on the ice skates they'd brought from
Holland.

On the muddy streets of New Amsterdam as many as 18 different languages could be heard as everyone went about doing what he or she had come here for — to make a buck. The Dutch were not interested in converting souls. The Dutch made no bones about the fact that they wanted a colony in order to make money. Fur hats were all the rage in Europe, and the Dutch knew they

See! How would you like it?

could make money if they could get their hands on a lot of beaver pelts. They built fur trading posts up and down the Hudson River in New York State, where all you could see for miles were Dutch people and very nervous beavers.

Meanwhile, the little Dutch colony of New Amsterdam wasn't doing very well. Drunken soldiers picked fights with one another and with the Lenapi, one of the main tribes of the Northeast. In 1642, Lenapi men, women, and children fleeing their Mohawk enemies ended up on Staten Island, which belonged to the Dutch. Even though the Lenapi and the Dutch had signed a peace treaty, the Dutch murdered the refugees. The Dutch women of New Amsterdam used the severed heads for a weird game of kickball on the dusty streets. Talk about horrible history!

Old Silvernails— A Law-and-Order Kind of Guy

In 1647, in an attempt to bring some order to the rowdy colony, the Dutch West Indies Company sent a new man to be in charge, Peter Stuyvesant. His nickname was "Old Silvernails" because of the silver nails that studded his wooden leg. A cannonball had taken off Stuyvesant's right leg in the West Indies.

Old Silvernails wasn't kidding about law and order. Stuyvesant *was* as tough as nails. He took over New Sweden and made it part of the Dutch colony. He started handing out fines for driving wagons too fast on Broadway. He closed the taverns at nine P.M. and banned drinking altogether on Sunday. He prohibited horse racing within the city limits; and forbade knife fighting in public.

The people of New Amsterdam didn't like Stuyvesant, and they especially didn't like the early tavern closings, which cut into their drinking time. However, for the first time, New Amsterdam began to grow. The settlement got its first school and first post office. Soon, the Dutch people were building brick houses with steep, gabled roofs like they had had in Holland.

The Dutch also liked things clean. They were famous for their cleanliness and their houses were very clean compared to those in other colonies. The Dutch whitewashed their walls and scrubbed their floors and sprinkled them with clean sand. The doors of the Dutch houses had a top and bottom so that you could open the top half for air without letting in the pigs, geese, and hens that roamed on the

New York

Sure, you can have a fight, just . . . not in front of the kids.

Contrasting
Colonies

KISSED HIS WIFE ON SUNDAY

Massachusetts

I guess this means no more reading their magazines.

roads. Almost every home had a bench outside built on a little platform called a *stoep* where neighbors could gather to gossip. Today, we still call this part of the house a stoop.

Making Money on Slaves and Wall Street

Peter Stuyvesant wanted the little colony to make money for its Dutch investors. Stuyvesant did everything he could to encourage the slave trade. Many Africans ended up living as slaves in New Amsterdam. They were put to work building the colony. The African-American slaves who

Wall Street and Broadway

Two of the most famous streets in New York City today got their names from the Dutch. Broadway was an ancient Native American hunting trail that the Dutch widened and called *Breede Wegh*. Wall Street is named after a 2,340-foot wall that Stuyvesant had built across the lower part of Manhattan to protect the colony from the English.

worked in New Amsterdam were often skilled workers: carpenters, blacksmiths, millers, horse trainers, gardeners, shipbuilders, iron forgers, printer's assistants, and doctor's apprentices. Under Dutch law, slaves had some rights. They had the right to sue in court, to start their own families, and to own their own land, usually out of town. In some cases, slaves were able to gain their freedom.

I'm worried about that guy.

Warrior   **Worrier**

Stuyvesant was a worrier. He worried about slave revolts. He worried about the Native Americans. He worried about all those English people moving into New England. Mostly,

Sweet and Rotten Teeth

The Dutch liked things sweet as well as clean. Without them we'd have no Cookie Monster, for the word cookie comes from the Dutch word *koekje,* and from them we also got doughnuts and waffles. It wasn't only the Dutch who liked sweet things. Sugar was expensive because it had to be imported, but the colonists in New York and New England learned to make maple sugar from the Native Americans. Almost all visitors to the colonies from Europe commented on how much the colonists loved sweets and what bad teeth they had. So many colonial people had rotten teeth that they stuck balls of cork called plumpers in their cheeks so they wouldn't look toothless.

Stuyvesant worried about the fact that his little colony had so few Dutch people in it. To Stuyvesant, the last straw came in September 1654. Twenty-three Jews arrived in New Amsterdam seeking to escape the Spanish Inquisition in

Brazil. Stuyvesant immediately sent a message by ship to his bosses at the Dutch West India Company in Amsterdam asking for permission to kick the Jews out. He insisted that "none of the Jewish nation be permitted to infest New Netherlands."

Back in Holland, the Dutch West India Company included several Jews on its company of directors. To Stuyvesant's shock, the directors told him to allow people of every faith to stay. The Jews held the first Jewish New Year's celebration in the United States in New Amsterdam on September 12, 1654.

Surrender Without a Drop of Blood

Holland and England were frequently at war. During one of their wars, on the morning of August 27, 1664, the people of New Amsterdam woke up to see four heavily armed British ships anchored in their harbor. Peter Stuyvesant climbed to the top of his fort on his peg leg and said, "I'd rather be carried to my grave than surrender."

The English sent the Dutch a letter saying that if the colony became English, everybody could keep doing business as usual, and nothing would really change. All they'd have to do was to live under the English flag. Unlike Stuyvesant, the rest of New Amsterdam decided that didn't sound so bad. Even Stuyvesant's own son refused to fight.

New Amsterdam surrendered without a drop of blood. Twelve days later it was renamed New York. Charles II, the newly restored King of England, gave it to his brother, the Duke of York, as a birthday present.

You're NOT going to guess what it is. Open your eyes!

New York City: The Growingest Town in America

Between 1664 and 1703 the population of the colony of New York grew from about 5,000 people to more than 20,000, with nearly 11,000 living in the town of New York itself. In 1699, the Royal Governor bragged that New York was "the growingest town in America."

New Jersey: Named for an Island with a Lot of Cows

In 1664, the Duke of York decided to give a chunk of *his* land to his friend, Sir George Carteret. Carteret was from the English island of Jersey, famous for its cows. The little colony of New Sweden was renamed New Jersey. Having lived through the religious civil war in England, Carteret was sick of fights about religion. He gave New Jersey a charter that said that any man could vote no matter what his religion.

Slave Revolts in New York

New York had the largest African population of the middle colonies. After the English took over in 1660, life became much tougher for all African-Americans. English laws were harsher than Dutch laws. In New York, a free African-American could no longer vote or go to court and testify against a white person.

In 1712, 25 African-American slaves set fire to an outhouse on the east side of Manhattan in New York. They ambushed the whites who came to put out the fire, killing nine of them. The New York judges said it was a "negro plot" to get back to Africa somehow. Twenty of the slaves were put

People do some terrible things to roaches, I figured it was because we're roaches. But people hurting people? That's crazy!

to death by hanging, but one was cooked over a slow fire.

In 1741, there were rumors of another "negro plot" in New York City. This time it caused a panic. A 17-year-old Irish indentured servant, Mary Burton, told wild tales about a slave rebellion being planned in the tavern where she worked. She named names, including those of prominent citizens who were helping the slaves. Burton was probably a hysterical liar, but, still, 200 people were accused and 70 of them confessed under torture. Medieval torture devices, which had been banned for decades against whites, were brought back and used on the African-American prisoners. Eighteen slaves and four white people were hanged; 13 African-Americans were burned at the stake.

Hey, Gov, Love Your Dress

Lord Cornbury, who was governor of New York from 1702 to 1708, was rumored to wear silk dresses and high heels and to jump out at bystanders from the bushes wearing his outfits. Some historians think these might have been rumors started by his enemies.

Pennsylvania: A New Home for Quakers

Remember the poor Quakers who could be hanged in Boston just for being a Quaker? Well, one person in England was determined that Quakers would have a place in America where they wouldn't be hanged for their beliefs. His name was William Penn, and Pennsylvania is named after him. William Penn's dad was an important admiral who had helped King Charles II get back his throne. Admiral Penn's father hated that his son William had become a Quaker. Still, William Penn was such a likable young man that in 1681 Charles II gave him a huge area of land and told him to name it Pennsylvania, in honor of his father. Pennsylvania was the last colony founded in the 17th century.

Equality, Quaker-style

William Penn sailed to America himself. Penn believed in extending brotherly love toward the Native Americans. He made treaties with them that he kept. In Penn's colony, any male could vote, no matter what his religion. Penn passed a law that made it almost impossible to

William Penn makes treats with Native Americans

Philadelphia, Pennsylvania. Franklin Court is the site of Ben Franklin's home in the 1760s. Much of colonial Philadelphia is part of **Independence National Historical Park,** and you can walk the streets where Franklin walked and visit the taverns that he hung out in. Just 16 miles outside of Philadelphia, you can visit **Pennsbury Manor,** William Penn's estate.

be thrown into prison if you were in debt. He even said that no person could be deprived of life, liberty, or property except by a fair trial by a jury of 12.

Quakers believed that everyone was equal in the sight of God, even equal to the king. As early as 1688, some Quakers protested that slavery was morally wrong and should be abolished. But they were not the majority, and Pennsylvania like other colonies had both slave owners and slave traders. Although some Quakers objected to slavery, William Penn wasn't one of them. He built a large estate for himself called Pennsbury Manor, where he kept slaves.

Philadelphia: The Jewel of Colonial Cities

William Penn named his colony's main city Philadelphia, which he got from two Greek words that, translated, mean "brotherly love." He not only named Philadelphia, he was the city planner. He laid out the city in blocks to form a grid.

He encouraged citizens to line the blocks with trees and he named the streets after the trees: Walnut, Pine, Chestnut. So if you live on a block that's named after a tree, the tradition was started in Philadelphia. In fact, if you live on a rectangular block, you probably owe it to William Penn's plans.

What Philly street would a school be on? Elemen-tree Street!

Philadelphia never had a starving time. The city grew quickly. By 1700, the population had reached more than 14,000 people. From the beginning, Philadelphia's houses were bigger and more comfortable than those in most other colonies. Many Philadelphians had houses with at least four rooms, each with a fireplace. Philadelphia houses also had the first windows that opened by pushing them up and down. (And yes, people probably did wash them with pee.)

Ben Franklin's Words to Live By

Publisher, inventor, philosopher, revolutionary Benjamin Franklin is still Philadelphia's favorite son, even though he wasn't born there. Philadelphia was Franklin's home base for most of his long life. Here are some sayings from his best-selling almanac:

- *Men and melons are hard to know.*
- *Fish and visitors smell in three days.*
- *The heart of a fool is his mouth, but the mouth of a wise man is in his heart.*
- *Early to bed, early to rise, makes a man healthy, wealthy, and wise.*
- *He that lives only upon hope, dies farting.*
- *He that lies down with dogs, shall rise up with fleas.*

Delaware: Thrown In with Pennsylvania

William Penn was not only granted Pennsylvania, his land grant also included what is now Delaware, named after the same Baron De La Warr who had helped rebuild Jamestown, Virginia. Lord De La Warr probably never even set foot in Delaware but a sea captain, swept off course in 1610, named the area for him. Delaware was first settled by Swedes, then taken over by the Dutch, and finally given to William Penn. But Swedish people were an independent lot. They asked William Penn for a separate char-

ter. He gave it to them, but they were supposed to remain in a "union" with Pennsylvania. After many arguments, Delaware got its own assembly, but it remained part of the Penn family's holdings until the American Revolution.

Maryland for Catholics *and* Protestants

In 1632, King Charles I of England gave his loyal Catholic friend, Sir George Calvert, two presents. He named him Baron of Baltimore so everyone now had to call him Lord Baltimore, and he gave him a gift of land in America, along the Potomac River.

Lord Baltimore named his colony Maryland. Some say it was named after the king's wife whose name was Henrietta Maria.

Others say he chose Mary because it was the name of Jesus' mother. Whatever the reason, the name stuck. Located on the Chesapeake Bay, right next to Virginia, Maryland is the most southern of the middle colonies. It was unique among the English colonies because it was a place where Catholics were welcome, unlike in colonial Virginia or in Puritan New England.

The Calvert family controlled Maryland. It was one of the best-run colonies that the English had. In 1649, Maryland passed the Toleration Act that granted both

No, no, no. I'm quite happy to tell you my religion. May I ask yours first?

123

How About Vote and Voice for Women?

Maryland was so tolerant that a woman even demanded the right to vote. In 1648, Margaret Brent was the first woman attorney in America. (She was also the first woman in Maryland to own land, some 70 acres, which she called "Sister's Freehold.") Brent became involved in all the major lawsuits in Maryland and was one of the Calvert family's most trusted advisers. She strode into the Maryland Assembly and pleaded for "vote and voice" for women. She was turned down — and it took nearly 300 more years for American women to get the right to vote!

Catholics and Protestants religious freedom. However, religious toleration in Maryland was *only* for people who believed in Jesus Christ. Jews or anyone else who didn't believe in Christ could be hanged. In fact, it was also a hanging offense to curse God. But, hey, it was a step toward religious freedom.

Tobacco and Plantation Life

Lord Calvert was one of England's richest lords, and he envisioned Maryland as a place like rural England, with large manors owned by a few wealthy planters. Tobacco grew almost as well in

Maryland as it did in Virginia, and it quickly became an important crop. Just as in Virginia, the plantations in Maryland depended on African slaves. When Maryland was first founded, Africans were allowed to earn their freedom, the way white indentured servants did. But as planters began making more money from tobacco, they believed they needed every slave they could get. In 1664, Maryland changed the law, requiring all slaves to serve for life.

Do you like

my new outfit? It's just a little something I threw together. I figured if the governor of New York can wear a dress, why can't I?

I'll tell you one thing though: It sure wasn't easy finding this dress in my size at the store. I had to fight off two grasshoppers and a plus-size ladybug just to try it on! Of course I had to have some alterations made. Dresses this fancy rarely come with six sleeves. The wig is a nice fit, though. Plenty of room underneath for my antennae.

Anyway, I can't believe those colonists were able to boss the Native Americans around while they were dressed like this. What could they possibly have said to them? "Do as I say or I'll suffocate you under 17 layers of my finest silk garment!" That doesn't sound very threatening to me. Even if they had a concealed weapon it would take them forever just to find it! Now, if you'll excuse me, I've got to practice my curtsy.

Chapter 5

Back to the South

From 1663 to 1732, the South got several new colonies. But the biggest change in the region was in the number of Africans. In some colonies, Africans outnumbered white colonists. Laws were changed to make life much harsher for the slaves. You might say, hey, slavery is so bad, how can it change for the worse? But it did. For most whites in the southern colonies, things changed for the better. The South had rich soil and a long growing season. Around 1700, some white colonists were becoming downright wealthy, and they couldn't wait to show off their fortunes.

TIME LINE

1663
Charter granted for the Carolinas

1676
Bacon's Rebellion in Virginia

1699
Williamsburg becomes capital of Virginia

1700
Slaves come in big numbers

1711–13
Tuscarora wars in North Carolina

Virginia Reels

In Virginia, the laws about slavery changed. Now, even if Africans came to America as Christians, they could not earn their freedom. Virginia became a colony of mostly farmers and their slaves.

In Virginia, towns like Jamestown stayed tiny because everyone who could, moved out and started a tobacco farm. Most of these farms were small. Traveling between farms and plantations was difficult. Taverns on the routes between farms became places where everyone would gather to gossip and find out what was new. The houses on the big plantations became the center of white social life, places where people would go to dance and meet one another. Wealthier Virginians were no longer living in little huts. They sent architects back to England to copy the designs of the finest houses, including libraries and ballrooms. Virginians took especially to dancing. One Virginian wrote, "We Virginians will dance or die."

1718	1732	1744
Blackbeard killed	Georgia founded; George Washington born in Virginia	Eliza Lucas Pinckney successfully grows indigo

Balls sometimes lasted three or four days and were important courting rituals. George Washington, born in Virginia in 1732, worried that he wasn't a good dancer. By the age of 16, he was already six feet tall. People who met him reported that Washington had the largest hands and feet they had ever seen. He worried that he scared the girls that he met and that he would trip over his big feet.

For most of the workers on the farms and plantations, there was little dancing or partying and no fancy clothes. Most colonists had only two or three sets of clothes. The poorer farmers in Virginia began to resent the rich with their big plantations and fancy balls. Sometimes they even revolted.

Fashion Statements of the Times: Buggin' Lips

White makeup and red lips and cheeks became all the fashion in the 18th century. Women applied white lead mixed with cornstarch to their faces, arms, and shoulders. To get red lips, they crushed an insect called a cochineal and rubbed the crushed bug on their mouths. They were definitely buggin' out!

Men were flashier dressers, wearing lace at their collars and cuffs. Men's breeches or pants went to the knee, below which they wore stockings of different colors. At dances, men would "make a leg," flexing their muscles in their calves to make them look bigger. Some were known to pad their stockings. After 1700, wigs became popular. If a man couldn't afford a whole wig, he'd just purchase the tail to add to his own hair. To make the wigs smell sweet, men would put a goo made of animal fat mixed with cinnamon and cloves on their wigs. (Think of how the bugs must have loved them!) Men had to be careful to stand up straight because if you lowered your head the wrong way, you could flip your wig. Very embarrassing. By the way, the word *blockhead* comes from the wooden heads that men used to keep their wigs in shape when they weren't wearing them.

YOU COMPARE

Fake cheeks?
Fake calves?
Fake hair?
Who could it be?

Hey, Nat, Your Bacon Is Frying

In 1676, a group living on the frontier in Virginia attacked Jamestown. They were a mix of farmers, poor whites, indentured servants, and slaves led by Nat Bacon. Bacon felt that the House of Burgesses in Virginia wasn't doing enough to protect them from the Native Americans on whose land they were living. This made Bacon sizzling mad. He and his army started their revolt by attacking peaceful Native American villages whose lands stood in their way. Bacon wrote *The Declaration of the People* in which he claimed that the government in England and the governors in Virginia were making poor people pay too many taxes and putting too many rich people in high places. Bacon and his army marched right into the fort at Jamestown and burned it down. Bacon died before he could be captured, but other rebels leaders were hanged.

Williamsburg:
A New and Fancier Capital

After Bacon's Rebellion, the Virginia colonists rebuilt the statehouse that Nat Bacon had torched, down, but then it burned down again. This time it was an accident. The colonists in Jamestown began to think that maybe they should move their capital. The mosquitoes that had bothered the first settlers had never gone away. The colonists decided to move eight miles away to a slightly drier spot. The new capital was named after the current English king, King William. In 1699, the town of Williamsburg became the capital of Virginia.

The colonists wanted their new capital to show that they were no longer worried about starving, the way they had been 80 years before. And they wanted to show off a little. They began work on an orderly town, with half-acre lots so that each house could have a garden with a fence. They built a magnificent brick governor's mansion with a ballroom, rich velvet draperies, Chinese wallpaper, and Oriental rugs. Outside the governor's mansion there was a bowling green and formal gardens, including a maze made out of hedges where rich colonists could

Occasionally, the groundskeepers would fill in the maze's exit so they could get a few hours of rest.

Williamsburg, Virginia, has been re-created as an 18th-century town. Every day there is a different day in history. One day you might meet Thomas Jefferson or George Washington or one of their slaves walking down the street. You can visit more than 100 restored buildings and can even get lost in the maze.

Tuscarora Fight to Get Out

The Tuscarora had been an important tribe in the Carolinas for centuries, most likely descended from the great cultures that had built huge pyramids along the Mississippi River. In 1709, the Tuscarora wanted to move their whole tribe to William Penn's colony because they heard he was treating Native Americans better. The North Carolina government refused to let them go, because they wanted to continue to trade with the Tuscarora and enslave as many of them as they could. Then, in 1710, a Swiss baron came to North Carolina and refused to even go through the silly pretense of "buying" land from the Tuscarora — he just took it. This was the last straw for the tribe. The Tuscarora attacked the baron's town of New Bern, killing 200 settlers, including 80 children. The women were forced to lie on the floor and had wooden frolic and get themselves lost. Of course, all these grounds had to be maintained by slaves.

North Carolina — Pirates' Delight

Carol is an old spelling of the names Charles. In 1663, King Charles II of England, the same king who gave New York to his brother, gave what would become North and South Carolina to a group of English lords. With the English firmly

stakes driven through their bodies. The slaughter took place in just two hours.

The colonists in North Carolina fought back for two years. The Tuscarora were outnumbered, and hundreds of them were killed and more than 400 sold into slavery. A peace treaty allowed the surviving Tuscarora to leave North Carolina. By this time they had begun negotiations with the Haudenosaunee who allowed them to become the sixth nation of their league. In 1722, the Tuscarora ended up settling in New York State, where they still live today.

Remember what I said a couple of pages back? Sometimes history really hurts.

established in Virginia, it seemed natural to them that they should push south.

North Carolina was a hilly land, not really suitable for big plantations. The people who moved there didn't really have much in common with the plantation world of Virginia (especially the part about wearing stinky wigs and putting crushed bugs on your lips). In North Carolina, the colonists were mostly small farmers who hated the penny-per-pound tax on tobacco. When a new governor tried to make sure that every penny was paid, the North Carolinians threw the governor in jail and began talking about having their own government.

If they couldn't get out of taxes by rebellion, they began to look for sneakier ways. One way to avoid taxes was to buy from a pirate. Pirates didn't pay attention to anybody's rules. If you buy from a pirate or, for that matter, from anybody who claims that something "just fell off a truck," you don't have to pay taxes on it. Of course, you are

Love Your Hairdo,
but Your Braids Are on Fire

Blackbeard was one of the most famous pirates in the Carolinas. Blackbeard, whose real name was Edward Teach, got his nickname from his charming habit of letting his hair and beard grow long, braiding both with ribbons, and then hanging lit fuses from his hat when he was going into battle. He also liked to drink a mix of gunpowder and strong liquor and light it. In 1718, Blackbeard lit his hat up for the last time. He wasn't easy to kill. It took 20 stabs with a knife and five shots to bring him down. Finally, his head was cut off and stuck on the ship's bowsprit. His body was thrown to the sharks. Legend has it that Blackbeard's body is still swimming around North Carolina looking for its lost head.

Trying to find my head?
Where do these crazy rumors
come from?
I'm just exercising to keep
my weight down.

breaking the law and can go to jail, but that's the risk of playing with pirates.

South Carolina: A Grower's Paradise — A Slave's Nightmare

The English lords who had been given the Carolinas decided that North Carolina was never going to be their best bet. They decided to put most of their money into South Carolina, which had richer land and a better chance for profit. Many of the settlers of South Carolina were English people who had lived in the West Indies. They were wealthy sophisticates who were used to owning slaves, lots of slaves, both Native American and African slaves. It was African slaves who taught the colonists in South Carolina how to grow rice, a crop that they had grown successfully in Africa. Year by year as the production of rice increased, so did the number of slaves. The African population grew so quickly that by 1700 there were four Africans for every white settler in South Carolina.

Rice was the gold of South Carolina the same way that tobacco had been for Virginia. Growing rice takes a tremendous amount of work. Rice plants had to be grown by reclaiming swamps, digging up cypress trees, sinking into swamp muck full of water moccasins and alligators. African slaves were forced to do all that

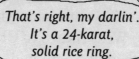

That's right, my darlin'. It's a 24-karat, solid rice ring.

work. When pirate ships started stealing Carolina's rice, Carolinians began cracking down on pirates.

Rice was not the only crop to grow well and make money from South Carolina's rich soil, 200-day growing season, and plenty of rainfall. Soon another agricultural product would become one of South Carolina's most profitable crops.

Rice was the gold of South Carolina.

Painting South Carolina Blue

Eliza Lucas Pinckney was a southern belle who inherited her father's South Carolina plantation. She was born in 1722 into a wealthy family in the West Indies. Pinckney spoke several languages and was a good musician, but what she loved most was to muck about in what she called the "vegetable" world. She loved to experiment with seeds.

Eliza was 16 years old when her family moved from the West Indies to Charleston, South Carolina. Charleston then had a population of about 7,000 people. Shortly after her arrival, her father had to go fight in one of England's many wars. Her mother was sick, so Eliza was left in charge of three plantations. She started experimenting with indigo seeds that her father had sent her. Indigo is the blue dye that became all the rage for dresses and men's coats.

Pinckney knew she could make a fortune if she could grow indigo successfully in South Carolina. The first crop failed, but she continued experimenting, keeping the best seeds. Finally,

When humans muck about in the vegetable world.

The evening began innocently enough, but everyone except the foolhardy Mr. Tomato Head knew, as they left the party, it could only end with him in a salad.

after four years of experiments, her crop was successful. She shared her seeds, and by 1747, indigo was making South Carolina's planters rich.

Slaves Do the Planting

Eliza Pinckney was unusual in that she taught her slaves to read. In South Carolina, most owners not only refused to teach slaves to read, they didn't even want them to be able to talk to one another. They were so fearful of slave revolts that owners would try to buy slaves from different parts of Africa so that their slaves wouldn't be able to communicate. Slave owners also forbade drumming because they feared it was a secret African code (and it often was).

In South Carolina, Africans got around those communications barriers by creating Gullah, a mixed language of both African and English words. We use many Gullah words today, such as gumbo for a soup made with okra, or juke as in jukebox. Some African words survived almost intact, especially if they sounded like English words. In Africa, girls born on Thursday were given the name Abba. In America, such girls were called Abby. In the Mende language of West Africa, *sasi* means prideful or boastful. It got put together with the English word *saucy*. Every time you sass somebody, you're using the mix of a Mende word from Africa and an old English word.

Escape to Florida

There *was* one route of escape for black slaves. In order to annoy their enemies the English, the Spaniards in Florida offered freedom to any slave who could escape from his or her English owners. If slaves owned by English colonists made it to Florida, they were free, and the Creek and Seminole tribes there welcomed them.

In 1739, in Stono, South Carolina, just outside of Charleston, a small group of African-Americans broke into a warehouse and got hold of guns. They marched south, headed for St. Augustine and freedom. They cried out "Liberty" as they went and other slaves joined them. The rebels were captured before they could reach

Fort Mose, a Free Fort

Stopping the Stono Rebellion didn't really stop slaves from escaping to Spanish Florida. In fact, so many slaves escaped to Florida that they were allowed to create their own town. In 1738, with the help of the Spaniards, African-American runaways built their own stone fort about two miles north of St. Augustine. Fort Mose was a four-sided fort surrounded by a ditch. Captain Francisco Menéndez, a former runaway slave from the Carolinas, was in charge. He had been born in the Mandinka area of Africa, and he commanded Fort Mose for 40 years.

Fort Mose, Florida.
You can watch archaeologists work at uncovering Fort Mose, just a few miles outside of St. Augustine. The fort is now a National Historic Landmark.

St. Augustine, and the heads of their leaders were put on poles to warn other African-Americans against thinking of another rebellion.

Curious Georgia — Too Good to Last

The English figured that the only way to stop slaves from escaping to Spanish Florida was to have a colony that stood between the Carolinas and Spanish Florida. In 1732, a very rich Englishman, General James Oglethorpe, got King George II to give him the land between Florida and South Carolina. Naturally he named it after George.

Oglethorpe was a very curious man. He had a terrible temper, and he always thought he was right. But he had some good ideas. He wanted a colony with no slaves, no worries about being thrown into jail if you couldn't pay your bills, a place where everybody owned about the same amount of land, and no one was rich or poor. No liquor, either, so nobody would get drunk. Sounds too good to be true, doesn't it? Well, it was, but that's the way General Oglethorpe started Georgia.

A good friend of Oglethorpe's had died in a debtor's prison. Oglethorpe hated the idea of people trapped in jail because they couldn't pay their debts, some staying in prison until they died. Why not send them to America? Oglethorpe didn't believe in slavery because he thought there was virtue in doing hard work for yourself. Oglethorpe and his first group of English settlers arrived in Georgia in 1732.

The first colonists were more farmer-soldiers than people who had been in prison. Oglethorpe got them to brave the mosquitoes and Georgia's steamy heat to build a string of wilderness forts against the Spaniards. Very soon after he founded the colony, Oglethorpe was leading Georgia troops on an attack on St. Augustine, Florida, when war was declared between England and Spain.

The War of Jenkins's Ear: 1735 to 1742

It probably is the silliest sounding war in all of history, but it was a real war, and it started with a real ear. Jenkins was an English seaman who was captured by the Spaniards and had his ear cut off. He saved his ear and managed to get back to England. He showed his ear, now all dried and shriveled, to the English parliament. The English declared that the Spaniards couldn't do that to one of them and declared war on Spain.

Oglethorpe again put on his English general's uniform. He marched his men on an attack on St. Augustine. In June 1740, they overran the little fort at Fort Mose, but most of the freed slaves

*A whole war?
An "ear for an ear"?
Wait a minute,
that's not right.*

145

escaped into the big Castillo of St. Augustine where they fought side by side with the Spanish troops. Oglethorpe bombarded St. Augustine for 38 days, but the massive fort with its walls made out of lime and seashells held. Oglethorpe and his men had to retreat.

The Spaniards then went on the attack, following Oglethorpe into Georgia. But in the Battle of Bloody Swamp on July 7, 1742, Oglethorpe ambushed the Spaniards. Two hundred Spaniards were killed, and Oglethorpe lost only one ranger.

King George II promoted Oglethorpe, but his Georgia colonists were not so impressed. They hated Oglethorpe's rules. They complained that they couldn't grow crops without slaves. They wanted to be able to buy rum. They wanted to be able to have larger farms.

By that time, Oglethorpe had lost nearly all his money. He gave up his colony. The king took it over and made it a royal colony, one that allowed slaves.

American: Anybody Know What That Means?

By 1750, nearly two million Europeans and Africans were living in the American colonies. There were 13 English colonies along the Atlantic seacoast. France claimed all the area around the Great Lakes, the Mississippi River, and the Ohio River valley. Spain claimed Florida and the West. The Europeans and their African slaves had built farms, plantations, cities with libraries, churches, outhouses, schools and let's not forget the taverns. Lots of taverns.

By the end of the Colonial Period, many of the colonists were calling themselves "American" because that was the name of the continent where they lived. But nobody really knew exactly what it meant. There was no typical American citizen (just as there still isn't in the 21st century).

The colonists were Swedes, English, Scots, Irish, Dutch, Germans, Finns, Africans, French, and Spanish. Mix that together with all the Native Americans and no other place on Earth had so many different kinds of people rubbing up against one another. Some historians think that

AMERICA
a human box-o-chocolates

not until we meet creatures from another planet will there be another such mix.

All these different groups in the colonies often fought one another worse than cats and dogs. And greater fights were just around the corner. The French were building more forts in the Ohio Valley and the English colonists were not going to like that one bit.

The colonial period lasted a little more than 200 years, about as long as the United States has existed as a nation. It was an amazingly bloody time, hardly a decade went by without a war. The colonists never had one religion or one king or queen to pull them together. They didn't think of themselves as a nation. Sometimes they felt more loyal to their city than their colony.

But after 200 years, many people in the colonies didn't think of themselves as belonging to the original place where they had come from, either. They didn't know exactly who they were. But they knew they were something different.

Can I be honest

with you? I think I looked better in the dress. This outfit? Pleeease! I look like I ran away and joined the circus. I can't believe what these colonists went through just to gussy up and go out dancing. I don't know why I bothered. The last time I went dancing, there was a strobe light above the dance floor that kept turning on and off. Since I have a tendency to run away every time a light turns on, I ended up looking like an idiot. Plus the only dance I've ever heard of is the jitterbug and I'm terrible at it. You might say I have six left feet. But enough about me. Let's talk about you.

Congratulations on finishing another great book! Keep up the good work. Oh, and don't worry about that George Washington guy. Something tells me he'll get used to his big feet and dance right into the next *America's Horrible Histories*. Bye!

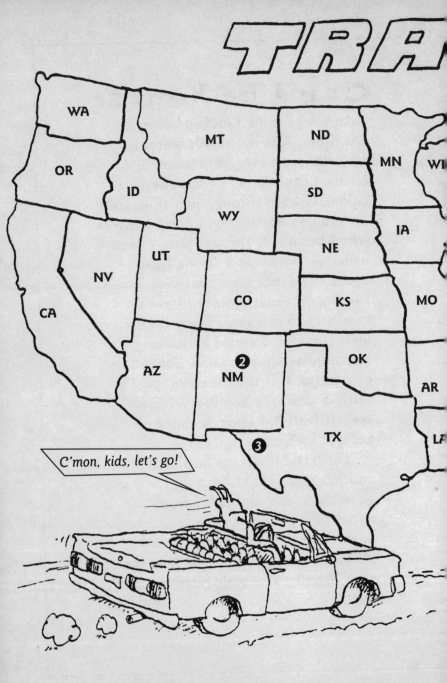

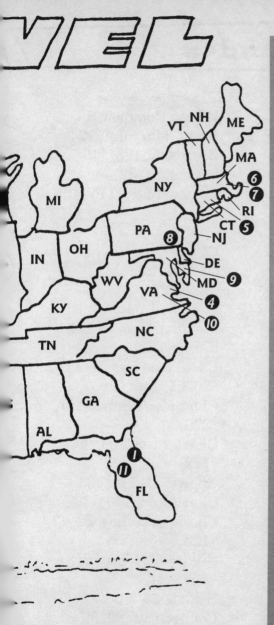

Index